KU-726-110

100 Indoor Plants

Their Care and Cultivation

revised edition in full colour

by

A. C. MULLER-IDZERDA

translated and edited by

VERA HIGGINS, M.A., V.M.H.

LONDON
BLANDFORD PRESS

First English edition September 1955
Second Impression April 1957
Third Impression April 1959
Fourth and Revised Edition 1962
Fifth and Revised Edition in colour 1966

From *100 Kamerplanten in kleur*
Published by N.V. Uitgeversmij. Kosmos

CONTENTS

Printed in Holland by The Ysel Press

Introduction by Vera Higgins

To be successful with plants in the house is very different from growing the same plants in a greenhouse; there the conditions are made to suit the plant, while in a room the temperature will be that preferred by the human inhabitants, the windows will be kept closed or opened to suit the owner, not the plants. But for those willing to take a little trouble, there are ways and means of combatting most difficulties. In the following pages the requirements of one hundred indoor plants of very different types are given and these directions will suggest methods by which other plants can be made to do well indoors also. Here a few generalizations may be given on the more important factors that must be taken into consideration such as containers, air, light, temperature, watering, soil and feeding.

Containers. From the horticultural point of view the ordinary flower-pots of unglazed clay are hard to beat, but they are not beautiful either in shape or colour. They can, of course, be hidden; the older method was to stand the red pot in a decorated one of china or metal, and now a number of newer types of outer pots or wire holders are available.

An alternative are pots made of glazed china or of plastic materials; these prevent evaporation through the sides, which is no great disadvantage in the dry air of a room, but it is essential that there should be a hole at the bottom through which excess water can drain away, for no plants grow well if their roots are in sour or stagnant soil. The drainage hole, however, raises another problem; in a living-room the surface on which the pot will stand must be protected. The obvious remedy is to stand the pot in a saucer but care must be taken that the drainage hole is not closed, and that the water which runs through is not left so that it is in contact with the bottom of the pot; the best way, when a saucer is used, is to have a low stand or to put in a few pebbles so that the base of the pot is always above the level of the water.

Air. Plants which come from hot dry countries will not object to the dry air of a living-room, but those from areas where the atmosphere is always moist will not do so well; a slightly moist atmosphere round the plant can be created by keeping it in a bowl of water, the pot being raised so that the water does not touch it; the slight, continual evaporation will have an appreciable effect on the air surrounding the plant without affecting the rest of the room.

Fresh air is desirable for healthy growth but is not always easy to provide. In good weather it is not difficult to open windows, at least for some period each day, but when it is cold and frosty outside, it is more difficult. This is one of the reasons why certain plants can be kept indoors for limited periods only.

Light. No green plant can grow entirely in the dark but the amount of light required depends on the type of plant and the natural environment from which it has come. Ferns and similar plants which normally grow in woods can be grown in parts of a room which are not well lighted; those that want a bright place are best on the window-sill as a rule, though it must be remembered that the sun at noon can be very hot, especially if it is shining through a glass window which is closed so that there is not much ventilation.

As a rule, growing plants should be turned from time to time to prevent them from being 'drawn' and growing unevenly; but when flower buds are forming, many plants dislike the direction of the light being altered and, at this stage, it is advisable to turn the plants as little as possible.

It is a good plan to stand the pot occasionally in a pail of water which comes about three-quarters of the way up the sides and leave it there until the upper surface begins to look moist.

Under natural conditions leaves are kept clean by rain and putting house plants out in a shower has much to recommend it but cannot, of course, be used for those kinds which must be kept warm, except perhaps in very hot weather. Instead, they can be sprayed and, as a rule, the water used should have the chill off or be about the same temperature as the room in which the plant is growing. Large, firm leaves can be sponged individually, an excellent way of removing dust and freshening up the plant. Spraying is needed by some plants which normally live in moist air; when spraying it is best to avoid getting water on the flowers as this is liable to damage them.

Soil. Provided the plant is healthy and has not outgrown its pot, there is little need to do anything. But should it begin to look sickly or when its roots are obviously getting cramped, then it should be put into a larger pot with fresh soil. For people who have no gardens and little space to store the materials required, it may be something of a problem to make up the various mixtures recommended. Suitable potting soil such as John Innes Potting Compost, is available in several grades and can usually be obtained from a florist or horticultural sundriesman. Special points to remember when repotting are: the new pot should be clean; it should have a drainage hole at the bottom over which a good layer of broken crocks must be placed; the roots of the plant should be carefully freed from most of the old soil. The roots should then be nicely spread out in the new pot and fresh soil, added little by little, evenly all round, and made fairly firm but not rammed down; it should not come up level with the rim of the pot but be half an inch or more lower so as to leave room for watering. For the majority of pot plants the soil should not be too heavy and either sand or peat or both can be added to lighten a heavy loam; neither of these materials contains any nourishment but both are useful in making the soil of a suitable consistency.

Feeding. Plants growing under natural conditions can send their roots out over a considerable area in search of food; those confined to pots are limited to a very small area and it is necessary to give them extra nourishment, by feeding it from time to time, particularly when it is growing freely. Organic or inorganic fertilizers are on the market, most of them intended to be used in solution, though sometimes they are applied in powder form. It is important to follow carefully the directions on the packet as an overdose may have serious consequences.

General Information

Plants requiring warmth but little or no sun

Indoor plants which want warm surroundings and prefer to grow in the shade also need a moist atmosphere. Spraying the plants and standing the pot on an inverted saucer in a bowl of water, so that the water does not touch the pot, will, in most cases, keep the surrounding air sufficiently moist. To spray the leaves themselves is not always satisfactory as, for example, with *Saintpaulia* (African Violet), *Sinningia (Gloxinia), Crossandra, Platycerium* (Staghorn Fern) and *Saxifraga sarmentosa.*

Sometimes in spring and summer the sun is too strong and shading is required, or possibly a sunless window is better. The behaviour of the plant will show which it prefers.

Shaded from the sun and in a warm environment, the following plants can be grown:

Achimenes
Adiantum (Maidenhair Fern)
Aechmea
Ananas (Bromeliad)
Anthurium (Flamingo Flower)
Aphelandra
Aralia elegantissima (Dizygotheca)
Asparagus
Asplenium nidus (Bird's Nest Fern)
Begonia rex
Billbergia (Bromeliad)
Blechnum (Fern)
Browallia
Brunfelsia
Calathea
Cissus antarctica
Cordyline
Crossandra
Cyperus (Umbrella Plant)
Dieffenbachia
Dracaena (Dragon Tree)
Episcia fulgida
Exacum
Fittonia
Gesneria
Manettia
Maranta
Microlepia (Fern)
Monstera deliciosa
Neoregelia (Bromeliad)
Nephrolepis (Fern)
Nidularium
Odontoglossum (Orchid)
Oplismenus
Pandanus
Paphiopedilum
Pellaea
Peperomia
Philodendron scandens
Phlepodium (Polypodium, Fern)
Piper nigrum (Black Pepper)
Platycerium bifurcatum (Stag-horn Fern)
Rhoicissus rhomboidea (climbing plant)
Ruellia (hanging plant)
Saintpaulia (African Violet)
Saxifraga sarmentosa tricolor
Schlumbergera
Scindapsus aureus (Pothos)
Sinningia (Gloxinia)
Streptocarpus
Strobilanthes
Syagrus weddellianus
Syngonium
Tillandsia (Bromeliad)
Vriesea (Bromeliad)
Zebrina (formerly Tradescantia)
Zygocactus (Christmas Cactus)

Propagating Indoor Plants

From Seed.

Some indoor plants can be propagated by seed. The easiest plants to deal with in this way are *Calceolaria* (Slipper Flower), *Capsicum annuum* (Ornamental Pepper), *Cineraria, Coleus* (Ornamental Nettle), *Cyclamen, Exacum, Primula malacoides, Primula obconica, Primula sinensis, Solanum capsicastrum* (Capsicum) and *Torena.* The method of treatment is given on the packets.

By Division.

Some plants can be divided when necessary, such as those where several stems come up through the soil, or which form a rootstock or where young plants arise round the base. This method can also be used for plants which separate easily into several pieces, such as *Anthurium* (Flamingo Flower), and *Primula sinensis*. Division of the root-stock is used for *Cyperus* (Umbrella Plant) and *Sansevieria.* Cut the stock into pieces with a sharp knife; on each piece there should be at least one shoot. Division of the root-stock can also be used for the reproduction of Ferns, Orchids, *Nertera depressa, Richardia* (Arum), *Tradescantia, Calathea, Maranta, Peperomia* and *Selaginella.* If possible, divide the ball of soil by hand, otherwise with a knife. If necessary, without damaging the roots, the ball of soil can be put into tepid water so that the roots can be carefully separated (*Anthurium, Calathea, Aloe,* etc.)

By Cuttings.

A job that amateurs can do is the propagation of plants by cuttings. For this, tips of side-shoots are generally used. The best time to take them is between March and the middle of September. As a general rule, the length of the cutting should be about 2-4 in. (6-10 cm). For large-leaved plants this can vary from 4-10 in. (10-25 cm.). The longer the cutting the more moisture is needed to make it root. Plants which can be rooted as cuttings when placed in a flask of water in a sunny room are;- *Begonia semperflorens, Begonia metallica* and other shrubby *Begonias, Coleus, Ficus elastica* (Rubber plant), *Fuchsia, Nerium oleander, Passiflora, Pilea, Plectranthus, Tradescantia.* As soon as they are rooted, pot them up in leaf-mould and sharp sand.

Other cuttings should be put into leaf-mould or peat with sharp sand. Before fertilizer is used, the roots should be well advanced; suitable materials are sold for this purpose, the cutting being dipped into the powdery material, having first been dipped in water, then it is put into a pot filled with soil; holes are made with a stick, into which the cuttings are placed up to the first leaves; press down and water. Cover with glass or a plastic bag. Put them in a warm room, but not in the sun. Where a stove or other form of heating is available, the plants can be put on a warm mantlepiece or on a coolish radiator. Under glass gives better control than under plastic where cuttings can be left for three or four weeks. Thereafter, water when necessary until new growth can be seen. Then gradually remove the plastic cover so that they are gradually accustomed to the dry air of the room.

This way of taking cuttings is, apart from the plants already mentioned, suitable for *Abutilon, Aeschynanthus, Aphelandra, Beloperone, Bougainvillea, Campanula isophylla* (Star of Bethlehem), *Cissus, Columnea, Crassula, Dipladenia, Ficus elastica, Ficus pumila, Hibiscus, Hoya, Ixora, Kalanchoe, Monstera deliciosa* (cut these below the aerial roots which should be wound round the lower end of the cutting), *Pelargonium (Geranium) Peperomia, Piper, Ruellia, Scindapsus, Sparmannia, Stephanotis* (Bridal Flower), *Syngonium.*

Layering

This is the name given when cuttings of plants with woody or square stems have the top cut off only partially, and the roots are first formed by means of help from the parent plant, before the whole can be self-supporting. Old specimens of *Ficus elastica, Fatshedera, Fatsia japonica* (Aralia), *Cordyline* and *Dracaena* are examples. A cut is made in the stem and the top, the part that is to be rooted, hangs down. Using a sharp knife, the cut in the stem is made upwards, about 1 in. (2 cm.) long, as far as the centre; or a ring can be cut round the stem through the bark, removing a circle about 1 in. (2 cm.) wide. The first method is the easier. Keep the cut open with a small wedge. Then smear the cut with glycerine mixed with fertilizer; cover this with damp sphagnum about 4 in. (10 cm) thick and bind it round with plastic tape. After a few weeks, remove and examine the cut. If necessary, moisten the sphagnum but the plastic covering round it will show if roots are penetrating the moss. Then remove the sphagnum, cut off the part below the roots and put the rooted part into a pot of soil. During this process do not water the plant itself so that the sap is kept as near the wound as possible.

Holiday Problems

The greatest problem for those without gardens is what to do with plants during the holiday period since, in the summer, they need fresh air and preferably rain water. If, there is no one to water the plants, they must, unfortunately, be removed from the window sill, for the more light and sunshine they get, the more evaporation there will be and this must be reduced as far as possible. Protection from the sun is essential. One means of guaranteeing a gradual supply of water is to put all the pots in the middle of the room, round a basin or pail of water. Into the water threads of wool or cotton or even fishing lines are placed and the other ends are put into the soil in the pots; two or three strands may be needed for the larger pots. Make furrows in the soil from the threads so that the water will syphon into appropriate places.

Another method for a smaller number of plants is to put each in a basin, the bottom of which is covered with a wet cloth in water about 1 in. deep. Damp newspaper under the pots also provides a moist atmosphere. A layer of crocks or broken brick covered with water which does not quite reach the pots is another way of keeping them moist.

The plants also want fresh air. If, without fear of burglars, an upper window can be left open, the problem is solved. Otherwise the door of the room can be left open and, before leaving, the rooms should be well ventilated.

Anyone who is away in warm weather would be well advised to soak the pots beforehand in a bucket of water, even over the rim of the pot, until it ceases to bubble. They then begin this difficult period with a good soaking and will be in better condition to withstand a dry period later.

For large plants, the pot can be wrapped in plastic which is tightly fastened round the stem, so that the soil remains moist. Tropical plants, which need a moist warmth, can be covered over with a plastic bag after they have been watered. They can be left like this for three or four weeks, but not in the sun. When the holiday is over, the plastic covering should be removed very slowly so that the plant becomes accustomed gradually to the drier air of the room.

ABUTILON

Attractive shrubs that remind one superficially of small Lime trees. There, however, the similarity ends for the leaf is smaller, generally five-cleft and toothed, while the flowers are bell-shaped. The leaf is often mottled with yellow or has a cream-coloured edge and, even if it does not flower, the Abutilon is a handsome indoor plant.

Now-a-days it is mostly *Abutilon hybridum* that are grown because they are more compact, for the other kinds may sometimes be as much as 5 ft. high. The flowers are bowl-shaped, so that the stamens in the centre can be easily seen.

The flowering time is in summer and autumn, but the plant may bloom throughout the winter in a fairly cool room or conservatory. The coloured varieties range from white, yellow, orange to red and sometimes the flowers are bicoloured.

Anyone who acquires a flowering plant in the summer should put it in a light, airy place but not in the mid-day sun; for example, in front of a window which, in favourable weather, is kept open all the time. Where there is a garden, it can be plunged out of doors in semi-shade, or the pot can be stood on a balcony, if this is not too sunny. Give it plenty of water when it is growing and flowering and, once a fortnight, fertilizer.

A plant that has been out of doors should be brought back again in October, into an unheated room or a greenhouse. Give it less water but, while it is still flowering, feed it well. During the winter keep it in a temperature of 50-55°F (10-13°C). Continue to feed it while the flowers last.

It is advisable to repot it every year, either at the end of February or in March. A good soil mixture is leaf-mould with old compost and sand (or broken brick). The pot used should not be too small and a layer of crocks should be placed at the bottom. At the same time it can be cut back so as to retain the shape of the plant.

The tips of the branches cut off, about 2½-4 in. (6-10 cm) long, can be used as cuttings; put them about 1 in. deep into small pots filled with leaf-mould and sand. They want to be in a warm place such as on a mantlepiece or radiator and, while the roots are forming, the pot should be covered with a glass jam jar and kept fairly moist. Instead of the glass jar, a plastic bag can be used as a covering; tie it tightly at the top, having first watered the pot. After three weeks see if the soil is moist enough, and after that it will only need the cover for another week. As soon as new growth begins, the cutting is rooted. Water can then be given more often and, as growth increases, a new and larger pot is needed, with the same soil mixture given above.

In order to keep the cutting shapely, pinch out the tips of some of the branches.

ACHIMENES

An herbaceous plant that, until recently, was almost unknown, is now offered as a striking, summer flowering plant. The large flowered Achimenes hybrid 'Paul Arnold' is said to flower throughout the summer months. The flowers are trumpet-shaped, violet in colour and beautiful in contrast with the bronze-coloured leaves. There are also other small-flowered hybrids of which the salmon-pink 'Little Beauty' is the best known.

The Achimenes are usually available as flowering plants in July and August, and the chief complaint is that they lose their flowers all too soon and seldom form more flower buds.

They drop their flowers well before they are over if they are in too sunny a place, or in a dry atmosphere, through too little light or lack of water. They grow well in a north window if the room is not too cold, otherwise they can be grown in a sunny room if shaded from the sun, for example, by putting paper between the window and the pot. The soil should be kept moist with tepid water and every fortnight fertilizer suitable for house plants should be given. A moist atmosphere can be provided by standing the pot on a support in a bowl of water so that the water does not touch the pot.

When the plant dies down in September, there is no need for alarm since the winter resting period is beginning, when the leaves dry up. The plant ceases to grow and can be kept completely dry in its pot during the winter at a temperature not below 45°F (8°C).

In February and March the tuberous roots are put into fresh soil, generally in a pot that is wider than high, with a good layer of crocks at the bottom. A soil rich in humus gives the best results, for example, leaf-mould or peat mixed with sharp sand. Depending on the size of the pot, 3-5-7 tubers are put in, about an inch deep. Use luke-warm water and a warm base to start them into growth and cover them with glass or plastic. A temperature of 65°F (18°C) is necessary for good development; for a good result 60°F (16-18°C) is sufficient.

The pot should remain under the plastic cover for three weeks and then be inspected. This is necessary, for the cover should not be removed until there are signs of new growth. Then gradually accustom the plants to the air in the room. From March onwards, shade from the sun and spray the plants with lukewarm water until the buds have formed.

ADIANTUM *Maidenhair Fern*

A fern unanimously recognised as one of the finest and most ornamental of the house plants is Adiantum, usually known as the Maidenhair Fern. Although universally admired, it needs more care than many plants do. The conditions under which the plant is grown are frequently rather unsuitable for, too often, it is used as a fill-up in a basket of flowers where it is impossible to give it proper care. It is best to remove it from the basket or bowl and to repot it; then there is a good chance that it can be saved.

It is better to buy a good plant from a nurseryman, such as *Adiantium cuneatum* variety 'Brilliant', which has coarse, wedge-shaped leaves, since this has proved the most satisfactory as a house plant. One might say that the smaller the leaf the more difficult it is to grow well in a room. A temperature of 65°F (18-20°C) gives good results.

What happens to many Adiantums when brought indoors? Most of them shrivel up, especially if put in the mid-day sun and, in the winter months, on account of the artificial heat. Every plant lover knows that they cannot stand a dry atmosphere. A moist atmosphere must therefore be provided, either by spraying several times a day or by standing the pot on an inverted saucer in a bowl of water. The new rubber bowls with ribs round the edge so that the water does not reach the pot itself are recommended. The plant should also be given plenty of water, several times a day whilst the plant itself is kept out of the sun. Rain water is best.

Some growers cut the plant right down in the winter and, when it begins to make new growth, it should be given liquid fertilizer, once a fortnight to produce a fine plant by the summer. If this method is not followed, it is still desirable to feed it regularly and it should be put in a light position, free from draughts, which it particularly dislikes.

Only repot when the plant has outgrown its pot and then do it in the spring, using a mixture of 3 parts good leaf-mould with 2 parts of compost and 1 part of sand. Where possible, pull the ball of soil apart gently, otherwise cut it in pieces. First put a layer of crocks at the bottom of the pot.

AECHMEA FULGENS *Bromeliad*

Not every Bromeliad is suitable for growing indoors but now-a-days more and more varieties are offered for sale which are well adapted to this purpose. One of the most suitable is *Aechmea fulgens,* with red, bead-like flowers tipped with blue. The variety *discolor,* with transversely striped leaves, is even prettier, whilst *Aechmea miniata* is very popular. The remarkable thing about a Bromeliad is that water can be poured into the rosettes and does not run away but is slowly absorbed by the plant without causing decay. In nature these plants catch the rain in these funnels and, even in our climate, especially in the summer months, they want it there too, as well as on the soil in the pot. In winter less water is needed and the soil should only be watered when it feels dry. Where there is central heating during the winter, water will also be needed in the funnel, but not when the plant is flowering. When growing and flowering, fertiliser can be given every fortnight.

As regards position, this Bromeliad is easily accomodated since it can stand either a sunny or a sunless window. In any case it should be shaded on hot summer days from the direct rays of the mid-day sun. It does, however, dislike considerable fluctuations of temperature and a constant temperature of about 65°F (18°C) suits it best. During the resting period, this can be reduced to 60°F (15°C).

After flowering the Bromeliad dies down but young plants are formed round the base of the plant which, when they have reached half the height of the mother plant, can be detached and potted separately in a porous mixture of 3 parts leaf mould, 1 part osmunda fibre and 1 part sphagnum moss. The old plant can also be cut out so that the young plants have room to grow, but, as yet, they have no roots. Put each in a small pot, otherwise they may rot off, and put a good layer of crocks at the bottom. If they need repotting later, wait till the spring.

ALOE

Aloes are succulent plants and natives of South Africa. They are often confused with the Agaves but they belong to the family *Liliaceae* whilst the Agaves belong to the *Amaryllidaceae*. *Agave americana* is the one most often confused and it is commonly known as the American Aloe or Century Plant.

Like other succulent plants, the Aloe can store water in its leaves. The skin is very thick, with few pores, so evaporation is therefore slight and the plant can withstand a long period of drought.

The inflorescence of the Aloe consists of a flowering stem which rises from centre of the rosette of leaves and carries clusters of little red and yellow flowers on branching stems. Flowering may begin in the winter.

Aloes need a light position in a sunny room where they can be shaded from the mid-day sun from May to September for the plants grow best in the morning sun. In spring and summer plenty of water is needed, but do not water them when the soil is dark in colour and feels soft. They should not be watered over the leaves since this may make them rot. Every fortnight from March to October give them fertilizer. Plenty of fresh air is desirable in spring and summer. Aloes can be overwintered in a cool, light, sunny place, not below 40°F (6°C). If kept in too warm a place the leaves tend to shrivel; 55°F (12°C) is a good temperature in winter. They need little water during this period, just enough to prevent the leaves from drying up.

In spring and summer Aloes increase by the formation of young shoots round the base. Detach these carefully and leave the broken surface to dry for at least a day; then put them into a mixture of leaf-mould and sand, or in peat and sand. Put the pot containing the cuttings into a larger pot filled with moist peat; this is an indirect method of watering and encourages the formation of roots without the risk of them rotting off. As soon as they have rooted put them into a larger pot, but young plants should not be put into pots too large for them, otherwise they may rot off. A good mixture is leaf-mould with good clay or loam, sharp sand and broken charcoal. Put crocks at the bottom of the pot.

Amongst the best known Aloes are *Aloe arborescens* (Tree Aloe). *Aloe mitriformis* (triangular, erect leaves), *Aloe striata* (Striped Aloe) and *Aloe variegata* (Partridge-breasted Aloe). The last forms offshoots from the base which, when they are large enough, can be removed from the plant when they are about 1 in. (2-3 cm) long. In the illustration, *Aloe arborescens* is on the left and *Agave americana* 'Marginata' on the right.

AMPELOPSIS BREVIPEDUNCULATA

A graceful climber with variegated leaves, which can also be used as a hanging plant, especially the variety *A. brevipedunculata* variety *elegans* which is particularly suitable for indoor cultivation. The leaves are very irregularly lobed and typically flecked with white and pink markings; sometimes the stems are also pink. The plant attaches itself by tendrils like the well-known tendrils of the vine.

Like all variegated plants it needs a light position to retain its beautiful colour. In summer it should be in the morning sun, if possible, for the mid-day sun is rather too hot. It shows to the best advantage with light from above, as in a glass-covered veranda where there is plenty of ventilation. There it will get enough space for the tendrils to hang free and not cling to other plants.

In summer give it plenty of water, but not if the soil is dark in colour and feels moist. Whilst it is growing, give it fertilizer once a fortnight. If it grows too freely, stop feeding.

In the autumn it loses its leaves and therefore its beauty, like the garden vine. Occasionally some of the leaves stay on depending on the situation but, in any case, it should rest in the winter months and therefore be given a warm place where it can be kept dry; at that time no feeding is necessary. During this period it need not remain in the living room, for it is now rather unsightly, but can be put in a light place where the temperature is 50-55°F (10-13°C). The cooler it is kept, the less water it will need.

At the end of February or beginning of March it should be pruned to keep it in check; this depends on how much space is available.

At the same time it should be repotted in 3 parts of good garden soil, 1 part leaf mould and 2 parts fertilizer together with some sharp sand; do not forget to put crocks at the bottom of the pot. But do not repot until the pot is full of roots. From then on it is given a warm position in the sun and the watering is increased. It should be shaded from the mid-day sun and, as the weather gets warmer, given plenty of fresh air.

Ampelopsis heterophylla is an earlier name of *Ampelopsis brevipedunculata*.

ANTHURIUM SCHERZERIANUM

Flamingo Flower

The decorative value of Anthurium lies chiefly in the beautifully coloured spathe; the flowers themselves are inconspicuous and attached to the quaintly twisted spadix which arises from the centre of the scarlet spathe. *Anthurium andreanum* (waxanthurium) is distinguished by the heart-shaped leaf and flowers like sealing wax, in shades of white, flesh-colour, pink, red and orange. An Anthurium may flower for several months and, since it does not need much attention, many amateurs are successful with this plant. A moist atmosphere is essential, so the pot should be stood on an inverted saucer in a bowl of water, the evaporation of which supplies the necessary humidity. The water should not reach the pot itself.

It needs a warm position in winter where the temperature does not fall below 60°F (15°C). *Anthurium andreanum* needs more heat, about 65°F (18-20°C). Regular watering is important, especially in the summer months, but too much water may cause rotting. Never use cold water. Sponge the leaves weekly, with rain water if possible. Whilst it is growing and flowering give fertilizer once a fortnight. It wants a very light position, in winter facing south, but care should be taken that in the summer it is not in full sun but either shaded by a curtain or in a room facing north.

Repotting will be needed every two to three years; use a mixture of leaf-mould and sphagnum, with fertilizer added. Do not plant too deeply so that the air can penetrate into the soil, and see that the drainage is good by using plenty of crocks. Cover the surface with a layer of living sphagnum to prevent drying out, but if the roots grow into it and are difficult to disentangle, put it in a pail of warm water to loosen them. After repotting, which should be done in February although, if it is still in flower, then as soon as it has finished, put it in a warm place, preferably at 70°F (20°C).

APHELANDRA

Aphelandra squarrosa, here illustrated, is the commonest, and is distinguished by the bright yellow flower spike above large green leaves with white, sunken veins. The inflorescence consists of overlapping bracts which enclose the small, yellow flowers. The variety 'Frits Prinzler' is much grown as well as the low-growing 'Dania'.

They are not the easiest of house plants but so much the greater is the satisfaction if one succeeds with them. As a rule an Aphelandra is in flower when received and then the object is to keep the plant in flower as long as possible. In nature it grows in damp, tropical forests and this means shading the plants from the sun. They can stand a good deal of light but, in a sunny room, it is best to protect them from direct sunlight by means of a curtain. As well as shade, an Aphelandra wants a warm, moist atmosphere, which can be obtained by standing the pot on a raised support in a bowl of water so that the water does not reach the pot. It is also a good thing to spray the leaves daily and once a week wipe the leaves with a sponge. A temperature of 65-75°F (18-25°C) gives the best results.

Whilst in flower it wants plenty of water, preferably at room temperature, and once a fortnight it should be given fertilizer.

After flowering, the flower-spike is cut off to encourage the formation of young shoots which will flower, though they will be rather smaller. The plant then wants to be rested for 4-6 weeks in a cooler place and less water should be given. It is possible that the leaves may dry up.

After the resting period the young shoots of the Aphelandra should be cut off, leaving three pairs of leaves. The plants can then be repotted in good soil, such as a mixture of leaf-mould and fertilizer, first putting crocks at the bottom of the pot. Then put it in a warm place and increase the watering.

The tips that have been cut off, about 4-6 in. (10-15 cm) long, can be rooted if put into leaf-mould and sharp sand. Cover with glass or a plastic bag and keep the base warm on a stove or radiator. Repot when growth has begun. Cuttings of Aphelandra can also be rooted in a bottle of water in a warm place which is not too light.

ARALIA ELEGANTISSIMA *Dizygotheca*

A fine plant related to the well-known Finger Plant *(Fatsia japonica)* which it does not resemble, this is, as the name indicates, more elegant in its habit of growth. But closer inspection shows that the way the leaflets are arranged resembles a hand with long fingers. The leaflets are narrow, long and sharply serrated, olive-green in colour with a reddish central vein.

On account of its habit, it can be used in a bowl with other contrasting plants but, as it develops into a pretty big plant, it is not suitable for small rooms or narrow window sills.

Otherwise the Aralia is a very sturdy plant, but less resistant to cold than the more familiar Finger Plant. It is best grown in a light room where it can be protected from the sun and given a moist atmosphere. If the pot is stood on a raised support in a bowl of water, so that the water does not reach the pot itself, there will be a moist atmosphere continuously round the plant. On warm days spraying the leaves is recommended, for in a dry atmosphere, this Aralia may be attacked by scale.

If this should happen, then the brown scales under which the insects are hidden can be treated with a brush dipped in methylated spirit. The following day they can be removed from the leaf with a mixture of soft soap and methylated spirit mixed with water; then sponge off with clean water.

An Aralia wants a good deal of water in summer and should be given fertilizer in spring and summer. In the winter it should be in a uniformly warm room, not below 60°F (15°C) and kept drier, since the roots may rot if they get too wet. In any case, do not water the soil if it is dark in colour and feels damp, and always use water at room temperature which, in the middle of winter, may be lukewarm.

Since it grows quickly, it would soon be a nuisance in a bowl with other plants so, as soon as it becomes too large for its neighbours, it should be potted up separately. This should be done in spring or early summer. Even a plant in a pot will soon outgrow its pot and, when the roots come out at the bottom, it is time for a larger one, but this should not be too big.

Since it likes an open compost, it should be grown in a mixture of leaf-mould and fertilizer. A good layer of crocks at the bottom is essential to prevent the roots rotting in the winter months.

ASPARAGUS *Ornamental Asparagus*

Clearly related to the vegetable are two kind of Asparagus which, on account of their fine, green, fern-like leaves, are incorrectly called 'ferns'.

Asparagus plumosus, which has the narrower leaves of the two, comes from the Cape and is used as green material with other flowers, in button-holes and bridal bouquets. *Asparagus sprengeri,* which has the larger leaves and comes from Natal, was formerly used for table decoration. It is now an indoor plant, particularly in window boxes. These Asparaguses differ in the leaves which are divided into small, needle-like segments.

Asparagus plumosus is the more tender of the two. It does not like dry, warm air nor full sun, which would turn the leaves yellow. A temperature of 55-60°F (12-15°C) is sufficient in winter. Water the soil with lukewarm water, and give no fertilizer; spray the plant with a syringe, otherwise the leaves will fall. In summer give it plenty of light and occasionally let it enjoy the rain. In spring and summer it wants a fair amount of water in the soil and should be given fertilizer once a fortnight. The plant does not need a large pot but, when the roots go through the bottom, it should be repotted. This is done in the spring and the ball of soil should not be broken but put into a pot one size larger, with crocks at the bottom and filled up round the ball of soil with leaf-mould mixed with fertilizer and some sharp sand added.

Asparagus sprengeri takes up more space but makes the better house plant because it is stronger. In winter grow it in a good light, otherwise it may lose its 'needles', and also keep it cool, at a temperature of 50°F (10°C) as a minimum. The cooler it is, the less water it needs but, now and then, spray the leaves. Water should never stand in the ornamental pot. In summer keep it out of the sun but give it plenty of fresh air. Sometimes in the summer months it can be hung in the veranda, when the colour will be better. Plenty of water is needed in summer and fertilizer every fortnight. When the weather is dry, spray it now and then and put it out in the rain occasionally. The ball of soil should never get completely dry or the 'needles' will turn yellow and fall off. If the water runs through the pot, stand it in a pail of water at room temperature, over the top of the pot and leave until it ceases to bubble. If well treated, older plants may bear little white flowers in summer, to be followed by red fruits.

Asparagus sprengeri forms thick roots and therefore wants a good sized pot. Put it in a large pot with good soil, then it will seldom need repotting. Large plants should eventually be split up and repotted in the soil mixture given above.

In dry weather red spider may attack it; for treatment, see under *Ficus elastica*.

ASPLENIUM NIDUS *Bird's Nest Fern*

Ferns are amongst the most popular foliage plants, for so many varieties lend themselves to indoor cultivation. Although they do not produce flowers, their graceful foliage more than compensates for this failing. In their natural surroundings ferns are accustomed to a damp atmosphere and a fairly high temperature, whilst they are usually screened from full sunlight. When these natural conditions are known, it is fairly easy to imitate them in the house.

The Bird's Nest Fern, *Asplenium nidus,* has a striking appearance with its large, shining, light green leaves, which are somewhat leathery and entire, in contrast to most kinds of fern. Down the centre of the leaf runs a strongly marked, dark brown vein which is especially well developed towards the base and on the back of the leaf. The arrangement of the leaves, as the name implies, somewhat resembles a bird's nest.

In summer it wants a lot of water, rain water if possible, otherwise it soon becomes very dull looking. The leaves should be sponged once a week throughout the year. If the plant is stood on an inverted saucer set in a bowl of water, the necessary atmospheric humidity will be provided and this is one of the chief requirements of this fern.

The warmer the place in which it stands, the more water it will need; otherwise a temperature of 60-70°F (16-20°C) is best. In a cooler atmosphere dark spots may develop. Most of these Bird's Nest Ferns do best if kept in the house, eventually the edges of the leaves turn brown, which is mostly the result of sun or a dry atmosphere, so spray the leaves several times a week. Cut out any ugly patches of rust and always retain a bit of the damaged part otherwise a wound will be formed which will go brown. In summer, give fertilizer weekly. A permanent position is much to be recommended otherwise, if moved often, they will droop.

If necessary the Bird's Nest Fern should be repotted in the spring in a mixture of three parts leaf-mould, one part peat and two parts fertilizer; do not press down too firmly because, in its natural surroundings, the plant lives in a well-aerated soil. Do not forget to put a layer of crocks at the bottom. Scale insects can be removed if the round, brown scales are touched with a brush dipped in methylated spirit. The following day remove them by syringing with a mixture of 1 litre water, 20 gr. soft soap and 10 gr. of methylated spirit. Repeat when necessary.

AZALEA INDICA *Rhododendron simsii*

If an Azalea is wanted to last for several years, no success will be obtained with the forced plants offered by florists at Christmas. Good plants which have been brought into flower at the normal time and are offered for sale from February onwards will last much longer; they are stronger and will probably flower year after year.

Begin by keeping the plant thoroughly moist, for the ball of soil may be dry; thereafter soak it once a week in tepid water. If the plant is kept out of the mid-day sun, the flowers will last longer.

Dead flowers and seed vessels should be removed. After flowering put the plant in a cool, preferably unheated room, give less water and no fertilizer, but see that the soil does not dry out. Spraying the leaves is recommended. After the middle of May, bring the plant back and, if necessary, repot it in a mixture of leaf-mould, peat, sharp sand and fertilizer. If well fed in the summer, an Azalea can remain in the same pot for several years. Plunge the pot in a sunny place in the garden or put it in a box of soil on a balcony or elsewhere, so long as it is in the open air. Usually growth and flowering is more luxurious if the plant is put into the ground without a pot, the soil being a mixture of leaf-mould, peat and fertilizer. It can then be repotted in September, using a pot that is wider than high and, if this is not possible, the ball of soil should be soaked in water and gently squeezed so that it fits in better.

In the summer the plant wants some attention. On dry days it should be hosed or sprayed and, once a fortnight, given fertilizer. This treatment should be continued until the end of September and then, when night frosts threaten, it should be brought into a sunny but unheated room. Whenever bright green shoots appear amongst the flower buds, pinch them out before they can take the nourishment intended for the plant when it flowers. Moreover, the flowers do not stand out so well among the new shoots which crowd them. Spray the plant regularly since this promotes the formation of buds, but not after they have begun to show colour.

The plant should be brought into the living room fairly soon, that is, when the buds are swelling, which is usually in December. Give it a light position and plenty of water and soak the pot every week.

For the treatment of diseases, see under *Azalea obtusa*.

AZALEA OBTUSA *Japanese Azalea*

One of the gayest flowering plants in the spring, from February to May, is the Japanese Azalea, with its decorative shape and wealth of delicately coloured, star-shaped flowers which almost hide the soft green leaves.

Many amateur gardeners manage to keep *Azalea indica* throughout the winter but generally do not try to keep the Japanese Azaleas, which look more delicate with their sparse foliage. Yet this delicate-looking shrub can not only be wintered successfully, but needs less warmth than *Azalea indica,* and can even be overwintered in the garden in a mixture of peat, leaf-mould and well-rotted manure.

One starts, naturally, with a flowering plant which must be kept moist but should not be sprayed when it is in flower as this is apt to damage the blossoms. If the water between the ball of soil and the pot tends to run over, the pot should be stood in a deep pail of water until it ceases to bubble. Dead flowers should be removed at once to conserve the strength of the plant. During the flowering period it should be given fertilizer every fortnight. When the plant has finished flowering, put it in a cool room, in front of a window, reduce the watering but take care that the soil never becomes dry, otherwise the plant will not flower the following spring.

After the middle of May, put the plant in a sunny position in the garden or in a box of soil on the balcony, in any case, in the open air. The plant must be looked after carefully, sprayed every day if there is no rain and given manure or fertilizer every fortnight. This treatment should be continued until the end of September when the plant is brought indoors again, put in the sun in a cool room and the foliage sprayed regularly until the buds begin to colour. Green shoots which develop amongst the flower buds should be removed since they develop at the expense of the flowers. As soon as the buds begin to form, more heat is needed. When the buds begin to colour, spraying should be discontinued but the soil still kept moist.

Waxy, swollen leaves covered with powder indicate blight. Damaged leaves should be removed at once before the powder (spores) has developed. These fungus diseases are spread by spores; dusting with sulphur will prevent it spreading.

BEGONIA 'EGES FAVOURITE'

Among the shrubby Begonias grown for their flowers, the winter-flowering, pink 'Gloire de Lorraine' is the original form, now superseded by 'Eges Favourite' and 'Marina', the flowers of which are less inclined to fall. Hybridisation between tuberous and shrubby Begonias has produced the large-flowered varieties. Unfortunately they are not strong plants and soon drop their flowers, and can hardly ever be kept from one season to the next since they have the characteristics of both the shrubby and the tuberous Begonias. 'Exquisite' is still one of the strongest and whenever this is grown in a very light but not too dry position near a window with morning or evening sun, it may then continue in flower for several months. A moderate amount of water and a dose of fertilizer once a fortnight will assist the flowering, but guard against too much heat.

The small-flowered Begonia 'Eges Favourite' is easier to handle if given a very sunny position, not behind a curtain, and not moved around more than is necessary. The plants like a rather moist atmosphere and a temperature of 60-70°F (15-20°C), plenty of water and letting it drain before the pot is returned to its saucer, is very beneficial. Sometimes they will flower for 8 months or a year, one after another. When the flowers are over, remove the old leaves and cut the plant down. Give it two or three weeks rest by reducing the amount of water and stop the feeding, after which the old treatment can be resumed. The plant is a gross feeder and repotting once a year is advisable, preferably after flowering, using a mixture of one part leaf-mould, one part peat and some sharp sand. Do not forget to put crocks over the drainage hole.

Begonias are apt to be attacked by mildew, which is best treated by dusting with flowers of sulphur, preferably at a high temperature 70°F (20-25°C). Repeat after 10-14 days and again later, if necessary. Do not spray a plant when in flower.

BEGONIA REX *Ornamental Foliage Begonia*

Among the house plants grown for their decorative foliage, *Begonia rex* has a special place. The name Begonia suggests a wealth of pink or red flowers but, in this plant, the leaves are the chief attraction and the tiny flowers should be removed to save the strength of the plant. Not all the plants will flower in the house.

The original Begonia is a native of the Himalayas and has large, asymetric leaves, green with a metallic sheen and a silvery edge. By means of hybridisation, the most gorgeous colour combinations have been obtained, the commonest being wine-red with silver and purple with grey.

The plant grows fast in summer and requires feeding so give it water regularly and fertilizer every fortnight. The plant likes light, but not direct sunlight, so that a position in a window facing north or north-east is best.

It may take a little trouble to overwinter the plant, not that they are so exacting, but in winter everything depends on the watering. The pot must never dry out but the plant needs very little water and, from October to April, no feeding. It can have plenty of light, in a warm place at about 60°F (16°C), and in a dry atmosphere.

The plant is propagated very easily and in a curious way; a leaf is cut off with a short bit of stalk and the veins on the back bruised or cut; it is then laid on a mixture of peat moss and sand and covered with a sheet of glass. New plants will form where the leaf has been damaged and these can later be potted up, in a mixture of equal parts of leaf-mould, fertilizer, peat and sharp sand. In this way the plants develop well, provided the leaf is in close contact with the soil. It can be kept down with small stones or held firm with a hairpin. July and August is the time, at a temperature of 70°F (20°C). Wipe the glass daily and at the same time give plenty of light to prevent rot. Instead of using a whole leaf, small pieces $\frac{1}{2}$ in. sq. ($1\frac{1}{2}$ by $1\frac{1}{2}$ cm), including one vein, can be used instead, and laid on sharp sand.

If the Begonia is *B.masoniana,* better known as 'Iron Cross', which has bright green, round leaves with brown markings, it needs more warmth.

BEGONIA SEMPERFLORENS

Amongst the annual Begonias is the small-flowered, compact *Begonia semperflorens,* a little plant with shining, round leaves and red, pink or white flowers which last for the greater part of the year. Certainly this is a good garden plant but it is also outstanding as a pot plant.

This Begonia needs a sunny, warm positon and plenty of water, with fertilizer every fortnight. During the summer give plenty of fresh air for they are really garden plants. They are usually in small pots when received and it is advisable to repot them at once, using good, florist's soil; above all do not use it too wet, otherwise the leaves will get too green. They are very free-flowering, especially the varieties 'Prima Donna' (carmine), and 'White Pearl', which flower all through the winter. Now-a-days there are varieties with double flowers, red or pink. In the summer they can easily be propagated by cuttings which should be put into small pots filled with sandy soil and shaded from the sun until they are rooted. They will also make roots in a bottle of water.

An entirely different type of Begonia, chiefly grown for its handsome leaves and which should not be overlooked, is the old fashioned Shrubby Begonia; the leaves are usually obliquely heartshaped, beautifully stippled and marked, and red on the underside. This lovely plant, which may be a yard high, produces in summer lovely hanging clusters of flowers, flesh-coloured or pink, according to the variety; the best known are:- *Begonia metallica, B. maculata, B. manicata, B. erythrophylla, B. scharffiana* and *B. haageana* 'Aalsmeers Glorie'. These plants are seldom seen at a florist's. Usually one acquires a cutting which can be rooted in a bottle of water in a sunny room. Later it should be potted in leaf-mould mixed with fertilizer and sharp sand. In summer give plenty of water and spray it on warm days and give it fertilizer every fortnight. In winter keep it in a heated room, not below 55-65°F (12-16°C) is recommended; give it plenty of water but no fertilizer and keep it in a moist atmosphere, otherwise the leaves may fall.

Leaves can also be lost through mildew. This should be treated with flowers of sulphur on a warm day. Repeat a week later, if necessary.

BELOPERONE GUTTATA *Shrimp Plant*

Among the newer house plants is Beloperone, which is called the Shrimp Plant, on account of the arrangement of its flowers, which is so curious that, once seen, it is never forgotten.

It is a shrubby plant with round, somewhat pointed leaves and the flowers themselves are white and quite inconspicuous but they are enclosed in coloured bracts, reddish brown shading to yellow so that the inflorescence looks like a hanging ear of corn.

From the shape it has acquired the name Shrimp Plant. For months on end, especially during the summer, this fine display can be enjoyed.

Beloperone can be brought through the winter quite easily; when it has ceased flowering, its appearance is less attractive, but this does not matter, for during the winter it wants a resting period and should, if possible, be put in a sunny room at a temperature of 55-60°F (12-15°C). Watering should be reduced to a minimum and feeding stopped altogether. As a result, the plant will lose all its leaves, which is its normal response to the resting period. In spring repot in good garden soil mixed with fertilizer and sharp sand; at the same time prune the plant to make it a good shape. More water should be given as soon as new growth appears and, if possible, put it in the same position it occupied the previous year.

In the spring cuttings can be taken which should be about 4-5 in. (6-10 cm) long; put them in a small pot containing peat covered with sharp sand, in a warm position but not in the sun; give it a plastic cover. After 3-4 weeks, inspect the cuttings and, if necessary, water them when new growth is observed.

A plant that is still flowering in the autumn can be overwintered in a warm room giving water at room temperature and, once a fortnight, fertilizer. Do not spray over the flowers.

BILLBERGIA NUTANS *Bromeliad*

Although comparatively few Bromeliads are used for indoor decoration, Billbergia makes a pleasing exception as it forms many new shoots so that young plants are obtained which can be distributed to other amateur growers.

Billbergia nutans, which is here illustrated, produces a number of narrow, dark green, stiff, leathery leaves, tubular in shape, whilst the hanging inflorescence is very striking, on account of the large, pointed, carmine bracts which protect the yellowish-green flowers.

The plant remains in flower for months, if properly treated. It must not have direct sunshine, especially during the flowering period in summer; it requires a lot of water, not only in the soil but also in the heart of the plant, for Bromeliads are able to store water for future use, since it does not run out nor cause rotting of the plant. On the contrary, Bromeliads take up water, not only through the roots, but also from the heart of the plant itself. Fertilizer should be given once a fortnight, Billbergias prefer a uniform temperature, preferably 55-60°F (12-16°C), in any case, a fairly warm position where the temperature does not fluctuate too much. In the winter much less water is needed; this is one of the few plants which can stand dry air due to central heating.

When it has finished flowering, the old plant dies but fortunately there are young shoots at the base which will make new plants. When they have reached half the height of the mother plant, they should be cut off, together with some of the roots, and potted up in a mixture of 3 parts leaf-mould, 1 part chopped sphagnum and one part osmunda fibre, and then there is every hope that the young plants will flower. A Bromeliad, that in nature grows on trees, makes only a small root system so that a small pot with a few crocks at the bottom is most suitable. Eventually the old plant can be thrown away and the young ones grow on undisturbed.

BOUGAINVILLEA

This climbing shrub came originally from South America but has now spread to all the tropical and subtropical countries. The variety *Bougainvillea glabra* variety *sanderiana,* with violet bracts, is now grown as a house plant and can be recommended for indoor cultivation. There are also pink, scarlet and salmon-coloured varieties, but they seem less satisfactory in the house.

Bougainvillea is one of the troublesome plants that soon lose their leaves and flowers in the house. The flowers themselves are inconspicuous but the lovely bracts, which look like butterflies, make the plant most attractive; the trouble is to make them stay on. Originally it was a summer flowerer, but can now be purchased in flower in the winter also.

If the plant is obtained in the winter, do not bring it into a warm, dry room straightaway, or it will lose its flowers in a week, but let it get acclimatised in an unheated, light, sunny greenhouse or a cool sunny room, at about 50-55°F (10-12°C), and give it tepid water. If the plant is not losing too many leaves, bring it gradually into a warmer place, about 60-70°F (16-20°C) watering it well and giving liquid fertilizer once a fortnight. After flowering, cut the plant back to keep it in good shape and to encourage the growth of new shoots. If necessary, repot in the spring, in rich soil such as turfy loam, leaf-mould and fertilizer. Then put it in a warmer, very sunny place and water it moderately at first.

A plant that has flowered in summer is cut down after flowering and wintered in a cool, light, sunny place. A moderately warm greenhouse or room is a good place to keep it in winter, and it should be given tepid water and no fertilizer. It may lose its leaves during the resting period. From January onwards it can be given more warmth and water and, when new growth appears, fertilizer once a week.

Spray the leaves daily until the flower buds begin to form. At the beginning of July or a little later, plunge it in the garden, choosing a very warm, sheltered spot or, if this is not possible, give it plenty of fresh air and a very light, sunny position indoors.

Sometimes greenfly makes it appearance; this can be dealt with by spraying with a mixture of soft soap and methylated spirit, or other mixtures recommended. It is also useful against red spider, recognisable by the yellow or brown colouring and sometimes by a web on the under side of the leaf.

BRUNFELSIA *Franciscea*

An exotic plant from Central and Southern America which is now used as a house plant. This is not an easy plant but the flowers are so distinct that one only has to see them once, to make every attempt to keep the plant. It has a shrubby type of growth and is related to the Ornamental Pepper. The leaves are oblong, light green and somewhat leathery and the flowers do not appear at a definite time but chiefly in spring or summer.

Brunfelsia calycina floribunda has large, sweetly scented flowers which are violet and lavender coloured.

In spring it wants plenty of fresh air but no sun. Whilst growing and flowering it needs plenty of water on the soil, and fertilizer every fortnight.

Anyone who has a garden can grow it out of doors successfully from June to September, either sunk in the ground or in a shady place out of the wind. It should be sprayed in dry weather and wants feeding every fortnight.

After flowering Brunfelsia wants one to four weeks rest, when it is put in a cooler place, given less water and no fertilizer. Later it likes a warmer position and to be pruned hard to keep it low and bushy. Whenever the plant seems to need attention it is advisable to repot it in fresh soil. Do not use too large a pot and put plenty of crocks at the bottom; shake the roots out of the old soil and repot the plant in a rich but light mixture, such as leaf-mould or woodland soil, with fine clay, fertilizer and plenty of sharp sand. Do not give too much water at first but, as it grows, give it more and then it can also be fed. In the winter it should not be kept too warm nor given too much water. If it is overfed during this period, it will flower badly or not at all. A temperature of 50°F (10°C) is sufficient.

However well it can be propagated by cuttings, this is not always successful in a room. When taken after the resting period, strong tips, about 4 in. (10 cm) long, will make good cuttings. They should be planted in small pots containing leaf-mould and sharp sand, put in a place out of the sun and covered with a sheet of glass, a glass jam jar or put in a plastic bag. Under glass they should be kept moderately moist. If wrapped in plastic, they need a good watering and then to be allowed to stand under the cover for three weeks before being watered again. When new growth appears, remove the covers gradually. Remove the tips once or twice to encourage branching.

CALCEOLARIA HYBRIDA *Slipper Flower*

Calceolaria is a curious plant which, from February to April, always attracts attention in florist's shops on account of the characteristics, bright-coloured and sometimes spotted, slipper-shaped flowers.

The plant is rather like a Cineraria in that it is also herbaceous and needs similar treatment, which means a moderate amount of water on the soil and spraying if the leaves are getting dry. It wants an airy position and plenty of light but not direct sunlight. In front of window facing north, in an unheated or only slightly warmed room, gives the best results. If the temperature is too high, it may be attacked by greenfly, the greatest enemy of this plant. As soon as this is discovered, spray with nicotine to prevent the trouble spreading. Then use a mixture of soft soap, methylated spirit and water. Repeat if necessary every 10-14 days.

In order to prolong the flowering period, artificial manure can be given once a fortnight, but not more often, or the delicate root system may suffer. Since Calceolaria is an annual, it cannot be kept over the winter; after flowering it dies and can only be thrown away.

It is possible to raise the plant from seed but, though interesting, it is not a simple job. The seeds are sown in June or July in a box filled with a mixture of peat and sand, gently pressed down but not covered with soil. Lay a sheet of glass on the top, keep in the shade and spray regularly to keep it evenly moist. When the plants are large enough to prick out, in September or October, pot them up, using small pots filled with a mixture of leaf-mould, fertilizer and sharp sand. They can be wintered in a cold frame or in an unheated greenhouse at a temperature of 40-50°F (5-9°C). At this stage the Calceolaria does not need much heat. When buds appear in the spring, bring it in to flower at a maximum temperature of 50°F (10°C). Shade them from the mid-day sun.

CAMPANULA ISOPHYLLA ALBA

Star of Bethlehem

Few summer flowering plants are so popular on the Continent as this Campanula which, from the end of July until late autumn, is covered with a mass of white, star-shaped flowers. There is also a pale mauve variety but this is not so strong a grower and needs more care in winter.

Although *Campanula isophylla* is essentially a hanging plant, it is often trained up a trellis or shaped into a pyramid. The natural form is, perhaps, the more graceful but not everyone has the space necessary for a hanging plants of such size, so that an erect shape must be adopted.

Provided the plant is given a permanent place with plenty of light, it makes an excellent indoor plant. It does not mind a north or a south aspect, but in the latter case, it will want more water, even as much as twice a day, while in a sunless window every two days will be found sufficient. Contrary to most plants, it prefers tap water containing lime.

The great thing to keep in mind is that a permanent place with maximum light is essential for strong, healthy growth and generous flowering. During the growing period, from March onwards until six weeks after flowering, it is essential to give fertilizer every fortnight. Dead flowers should be removed.

In winter the stems are cut back to one pair of leaves above the soil, then put the plant into a cool, sunny place at 40-50°F (5-10°C), where it needs very little water. If necessary, repot in the spring in a mixture of 2 parts leaf-mould, 1 part fertilizer or old compost and 1 part sharp sand.

The tops cut off and reduced to a length of 3-4 in. (6-10 cm) can be used for propagation; they should be put into moist leaf-mould and sharp sand and covered with glass or plastic. Cuttings taken in May should flower the same summer. It is better to put 3 to 5 cuttings in a pot, rather than only one, as this produces a larger plant more quickly. If they do not branch, the tips can be removed, which will make them break.

If the leaves begin to turn yellow and this is not due to lack of water or being in full sun, red spider may be the cause. Spray with a suitable insecticide.

CEROPEGIA WOODII

Chinese Lantern Plant

An attractive little hanging plant that belongs to the succulent group, although it does not look very succulent, with its slender stems and kidney-shaped leaves, growing in pairs at long intervals up the stem.

Closer inspection will show that the dark green leaves, marbled with white, are fleshy but the plant has the unusual characteristic in that it produces little tubers in the axils of the leaves; below the soil the plant is also tuberous. In the summer the typical lantern-shaped, little flowers appear, whitish pink in colour. They are not especially striking but their amusing shape distinguishes them from other flowers. It is a good house plant, useful against a wall or to hang down from the top of a book case or cupboard, where its slender stems can hang freely without getting tangled. Although it does not need sunshine, it grows much better in a sunny place. If it grows too freely, starve it a little.

Do not give it much water in summer or winter, especially if the soil feels damp. In the growing period fertilizer may be given every fortnight. In winter put it in a sunny, cool place but it will not stand frost. A moderately warm room is best; it does not mind dry air.

If it grows out of its pot, repot it in the spring; the soil used is not very important, but leaf-mould with loam and sharp sand gives good results. After repotting, keep it out of the sun for the first week and water sparingly. It is easily propagated by tubers from the leaf-axils which soon root in a pot in damp leafmould and sand. A glass jam jar or a plastic bag over the pot speeds up the rooting. Give it a warm place but not in the sun. Propagation can be carried out either in spring or summer, but the spring is the better time as the cuttings root more quickly then.

This Ceropegia can be grown from seed also. The seed is found in the pod-like fruits and, when sown in a warm, moist atmosphere, under glass, it germinates very quickly.

CHLOROPHYTUM *Phalangium*

One of the best known and, at the same time, the sturdiest of hanging plants suitable for indoor cultivation is the variegated Phalangium whose Latin name is *Chlorophytum comosum variegatum.* The long, ribbon-like leaves are edged with white and the remarkable feature is that it does not become a hanging plant until it has flowered. Only a strong, healthy plant will produce flowers. Long stalks emerge from the centre of the plant, which bear little, inconspicuous white flowers; when these fade they should be removed at once, but the stalk is allowed to remain as the young plants develop along it. Then the plant has become a hanging plant, the stems arch over under the weight, bending lower and lower until the plant has an entirely different appearance from that shown in the illustration.

As an indoor plant it is extraordinarily easy to keep, for it will grow in any soil, in any position and in any temperature. When it gets plenty of light, the white edges of the leaves will be much more marked than if in a shadier position, where the white edges may disappear and the leaves become a uniform green. In summer the plant likes a place where it gets the morning sun, or before a sunless window; in any case it does not want to be too warm but to have plenty of air.

Brown, withered leaf tips suggest that it has had too much sun, a dry atmosphere or damage. Cut them off but leave about 1 mm so as not to make a wound. Dull, greyish leaves suggest red spider; spray them with a insecticide. After 10-14 days, repeat if necessary.

In summer it wants plenty of water in the soil and it is as well to spray the leaves and occasionally to sponge them. Now and then put the plant out in the rain. Every fortnight give it fertilizer. When it gets too large for its pot, put it in a bigger one in the spring, with a mixture of leaf-mould, turf and fertilizer.

It is easily propagated from the plantlets that develop on the flower stalks. These are already forming roots and begin to grow as soon as they are potted up. It goes without saying that, in this way, many young plants can be obtained.

CINERARIA *Senecio cruentus*

As regards the treatment of the Cineraria, whose name is actually *Senecio cruentus,* this is more difficult than one would expect, but why not give it the care it needs since thereby its life can be considerably prolonged.

It is an herbaceous plant whose leaves want plenty of moisture and, at the same time, a cool position. But all too often Cinerarias are seen in full sun, the leaves curled up and dry, drooping lifelessly so that the plant has lost all its charm.

Cinerarias want a place out of direct sunshine where the heat of the fire or stove cannot reach them, otherwise they may be attacked by greenfly which makes its appearance very suddenly. These insects should be sprayed with a mixture of soft soap, methylated spirit and water. Prevention is always better than cure. A sunless window in a cool room, regular watering and spraying the leaves occasionally, all tend to build up a healthy, long-flowering plant. Give sufficient water and do not water again until the soil is dry. Spray the leaves regularly; if they go limp, then put the pot in a pail of water until it ceases to bubble. The leaves want sponging daily and the flowers will last longer if fertilizer is given once a week.

When the flowers are over, an attempt should be made to propagate the plant by cuttings. If it is put out of doors, young plantlets will form at the base; these can be detached in September and potted up in loam and well-rotted manure. Keep them in a cool greenhouse or frost-free room at a temperature of 50°F (10°C).

The great attraction of these plants lies in the uncommon colours which are not found in other house plants, such as dark blue, cornflower blue, azure, turquoise blue, blue with a white centre, pink, flesh-coloured, coppery-scarlet, in various tones. These marvellous colours may well compensate for the plant's short span of life. The varieties are well-known as hybrids of *Senecio cruentus.* The best have been derived from *Senecio cruentus multiflora nana* with the most extensive range of colours.

Before sowing Cinerarias, refer to the method given under *Calceolaria.*

CISSUS ANTARCTICA

This climber, which is very popular in Scandinavian countries, belongs to the vine family and is, therefore, related to the grape. The tendrils show that it is a climbing plant. The leaves are pale green and resemble a beech leaf. It is best grown in a semi-circular wall pot which has a flat back. The plant will cling to the wall on its own but it grows larger, and then a few drawing pins with hooks attached may be needed to guide it.

It is not necessary to put this plant in front of a window for it does not like sun. It does very well in a room facing north or north-east, where it can stand a yard or more away from the window. In a darker place the leaves become larger. In summer give it plenty of water and in winter rather less; but never water it if the soil is dark in colour. Once a month give it fertilizer. If the leaves get dusty, spray them or put the plant out in the rain. In the autumn it can be put in an unheated room but beware of frost. On the other hand it can stand a good deal of heat and may be put on the mantlepiece or near the radiator. In the spring it can be propagated by means of top or side shoots put in sandy soil and leaf-mould, in a warm place preferably under glass or wrapped in plastic, where it will soon begin to grow. Under glass keep it fairly moist and, if in plastic, it is usual to water it well and then leave it for three weeks. When growth has begun, pot the cuttings up in a mixture of 3 parts leaf-mould, 2 parts fertilizer and 1 part sharp sand.

Another variety is *Cissus rhombifolia (Rhoicissus rhomboidea)* with tripartite, diamond-shaped leaves, more like a Virginia Creeper but smaller. The colouring is attractive, being green above and reddish below.

A later introduction is *Cissus striata (Ampelopsis henryanum)* with a five-partite leaf which resembles *Rhoicissus* but is much smaller.

Sometimes, as a result of dry, winter warmth, red spider may appear, recognisable by the yellow or brown discoloration of the leaves, occasionally with the web on the underside of the leaves. Spray it with an insecticide. Repeat 10-14 days later or whenever necessary. Do not forget to treat the back of the leaf also.

CLIVIA

One of our older foliage plants, Clivia is useful also for decoration in the modern setting, with its symmetrical habit and striking orange flowers. During the flowering period, which lasts for weeks, Clivia should be put in a light position in a warm room where sunshine will do it no harm. Later, in spring and summer, it is better to put it near a window which gets no sun since full sun may cause brown marks on the leaves. Whilst it is in flower give it plenty of water and, once a week, fertilizer. When the flowers are over, cut the flower stalks as low down as possible, so as not to take too much strength from the plant. The remains of the flower stem should be pulled out as soon as it has dried up, Some people leave the flower heads on so as to enjoy the fruits which may remain on the plant for a year. When they fall off, the ripe seeds within them can be sown in small pots of leaf-mould. After flowering the real growth of the plant begins and then it wants plenty of nourishment, so give it water and fertilizer; the leaves should be sponged weekly with tepid water. A Clivia that has been well looked after may produce 4-6 new leaves in one year.

In November the resting period begins, and then it must be kept quiescent while the flower buds are forming, so very little water should be given, the feeding stopped and the plant put in a sunny place at a temperature of 50°F (8-10°C). When the flower buds appear, give it a warmer place, about 60-65°F (16-18°C), but do not water until the flower stalks are 6 in. (15 cm) long. When the roots appear on the surface of the soil, it should be repotted; this may be needed every two to three years. The new pot should be only one size larger and the soil mixture should consist of equal parts of leaf-mould, loam, well-rotted manure or fertilizer, and sharp sand. Young offsets should be removed with a few roots and potted up. If they are taken too soon from the mother plant and have no roots they are rarely successful. When bits of white fluff can be seen in the centre, the plant is being attacked by lice. The fluff should be removed bit by bit with a brush dipped in methylated spirit and soft soap and water, or other suitable insecticide.

CODIAEUM VARIEGATUM *Croton*

A coloured foliage plant which comes from Indonesia and, in this country, is only really successful in a warm, moist greenhouse.

It is included now-a-days among the house plants because it is frequently used in decorative bowls on account of its lovely colour.

The type here illustrated is the one most usually grown and there are also kinds with oval, linear and even 3-lobed leaves (like oak leaves). The thick leathery leaves are sometimes yellow veined with red, or green veined with yellow or flecked, then again it is green with red or purple markings.

To retain the colour, the plant needs plenty of light and sun. Only occasionally on warm summer days should it be shaded from full sun at mid-day. In the house it soon loses its leaves either on account of the dry warmth of the room or because it is too cool for it. Because of its tropical origin it needs a warm, moist atmosphere. It can be overwintered in a centrally heated room with a very high, uniform temperature. If the heating is by means of a stove, it is more difficult but on a warm mantlepiece it has a better chance.

The moist atmosphere is provided by standing the pot on a raised support in a bowl of water so that the water does not touch the pot, or by putting the pot into a decorative one and packing the space between with sphagnum moss which is moistened weekly. The leaves should be sprayed daily or, if this is not possible, at least sponged weekly.

Codiaeums need a lot of water on the soil which should be at least at room temperature or, in winter, luke warm. In spring and summer they can be given fertilizer every fortnight.

The plant is apt to be attacked by mealy bug, mostly in the axils of the leaves; this is recognised by the white, fluffy covering that protects the insects. They can be destroyed by touching each with a brush, dipped in a mixture of methylated spirit and soft soap in water.

Codiaeums should, if they have outgrown their pots, be repotted in the spring, about April or May, using a pot which is not much larger. The compost should consist of leaf-mould with turfy loam and fertilizer, equal parts of each. Do not forget to cover the hole with crocks.

COLEUS *Ornamental Nettle*

Although most plants prefer a cool place in summer, either in a garden or in the house, with little or no sun, there are a few exceptions, and the one that immediately comes to mind is Coleus or the Ornamental Nettle whose foliage is multi-coloured and which enjoys the heat of the sun. Fortunately this Ornamental Nettle, with its brightly coloured leaves, has nothing in common with the Stinging Nettle, except its shape and is, in fact, an ideal house plant. It goes without saying that a plant which can develop into a show specimen in one year, needs a lot of feeding and this is supplied by giving liberal doses of water, and fertilizer once a week.

If a Coleus does not get enough water it immediately droops, which is often thought to be due to the hot sun, but sunshine is what the plant chiefly needs. Soaking in a pail of water soon revives it, but prevention is better than cure, so it should be watered twice a day in really hot weather. The plant also needs plenty of fresh air in the summer.

A rapid grower like Coleus will soon want a larger pot; replant in a mixture of 3 parts leaf-mould, 2 parts fertilizer and 1 part sharp sand.

Although the plant is generally raised from seed, it can usually be kept through the winter in a warm, light place, at 60-65°F (16-18°C) and the small-leaved *Coleus rehneltianus* may live for several years. The largest leaved, *Coleus hybrida,* grows rather untidy after a time and, in winter, becomes bare at the base owing to the warm, dry air. In that case it is better to take the leafy tips off in the spring, about 3-4 in. (6-10 cm) long, and treat them as cuttings whilst the old plant is thrown away. The cuttings root quickly in a jar of water in a sunny room. When they have rooted, pot them up in the soil mixture given above. Remove some of the tips to make the plant branch.

As the small flower clusters appear, remove most of them for they are inconspicuous and take too much nourishment from the plant.

Greenfly may attack the plant and then it should be sprayed with a mixture of soft soap, methylated spirit and water. Repeat after 10-14 days, if necessary. Do not forget the underside of the leaves.

COLUMNEA

A hanging plant from tropical America which, not so long ago, would have been found only in the hot houses of botanical gardens. But now it can be purchased in a florist's shop and has come into our rooms almost unnoticed. It is always a success there, but that is another matter and it may be useful to give the treatment it requires.

This hanging plant, related to *Gloxinia* and *Gesneria,* has long branches with pairs of velvety, grey-green leaves against which the butterfly-like, scarlet, tubular flowers stand out. The flowers resemble those of a *Gesneria* but are looser, more open and have a yellow throat. They generally appear in spring or summer, but vary according to the warmth and water content of their surroundings.

Columnea is an epiphyte which in nature grows on trees and so should be given a shady place in the house and a warm, moist atmosphere; the soil used should be open.

Put the plant in the warmest room available, one facing south or south-west, but shaded from the mid-day sun in spring and summer.

During the flowering season give it plenty of water which should be at room temperature, with fertilizer every fortnight. The branches may grow to a length of 2-3 ft. (60-80 cm). The moist atmosphere round the plant can be produced by putting the pot on a stand in a bowl of water so that the water does not reach the bottom of the pot. It is advisable to spray the plants on warm days using rain water if possible. As soon as the flowers are over, the stems can be cut back, which encourages branching, and ultimately more branches will produce flowers.

In winter it should be put in a warm room where it will need little water and no fertilizer. Keep it quite dry for one month. When it is well fed for the rest of the year it will seldom need repotting, but if the Columnea outgrows its pot, it should be repotted in the spring in an open mixture of leaf-mould, peat and and sharp sand, or leaf-mould with fertilizer and sphagnum. To keep the soil open, a good layer of crocks should be put at the bottom. After repotting, put it in a warm place at about 65°F (18-20°C), out of the sun and at first water sparingly.

CRASSULA FALCATA

In the summer months the window sill is apt to be rather empty since many plants are put out in the garden or on the balcony, so that it is a luxury to have a flowering plant in the house at that time.

Such a plant is *Crassula falcata,* already well known as a foliage plant, with its fleshy, sickle-shaped, velvety grey coloured leaves, arranged in pairs opposite each other and embracing the stem. This plant takes up a good deal of space with its spreading leaves and may reach a height of 1½-2 ft. (40-50 cm). The plant used to be sold as *Rochea falcata* by nurserymen, under which erroneous name it is still sometimes found.

In July the flowers are produced in a bright red umbel above the leaves. Before and during flowering it wants a lot of water but in winter the watering can be gradually reduced and it can be given a bright, cool place. From March to October it should be given fertilizer every fortnight. A temperature of 40°F (4-6°C) is sufficient. Put it in full sun both in summer and winter.

The best way to propagate the plant is by cuttings, but since the plant is succulent, it is advisable to leave the cuttings to dry for some hours before planting them, so as to prevent rotting. The cuttings can be taken from top or side shoots and also from leaves which are removed with a small piece of stem. Put them in a mixture of fine sand and peat where they will root quickly. Being succulent plants they want a small pot with plenty of crocks at the bottom and when they outgrow the pot, repot them in the spring, using a mixture of leaf-mould, loam and fertilizer, for this Crassula will not thrive in poor soil.

In summer it can be put in the garden, in a sunny, sheltered place, pot and all, but it should be brought in again at the end of September. In the house the plant wants plenty of light.

CROSSANDRA

Among the newer house plants is *Crossandra ifundibuliformis,* an elaborate name for this small plant which is better known as *Crossandra undulaefolia.* This shrub comes from Indonesia; it has large, pointed, leathery leaves and an inflorescence like an ear of corn. The colour is a lovely orange and the flowers are slanting with a long flower tube. They are produced in the axils of green, scale-like bracts.

Reluctantly it made its appearance in Holland, not on account of its appearance alone, which is striking enough, but probably because in the house it drops its flowers and growers did not recommend it. Now it has been fully tested and turns out to be especially beautiful, together with the violet *Saintpaulia,* with which it harmonises in colour and height extremely well.

Anyone who gets a Crossandra should put the plant on a window sill which is shaded from the mid-day sun. A temperature of at least 65°F (18°C) gives the best results. If the window faces south, it will be all right provided a sheet of paper is put between the window and the pot in sunny weather. From force of habit we give plenty of water to a tropical plant and spray it overhead on hot days, but with Crossandra this is not necessary. It will not stand too much water in the soil, and it should never be cold. Water only when the soil is light in colour and dry, and never spray over the leaves for, if too moist and in a moist atmosphere, the leaves fall and rot may set in.

During growth and flowering a dose of fertilizer once a fortnight is desirable so that the flowers may last longer. If well treated and kept in the same position, Crossandra can be kept in flower from May or June to September or October.

In winter they need moderate warmth, not below 50°F (12°C) would be suitable. During that period they do not need much water and this should be tepid; fertilizer should not be given until February or March. Avoid draughts, especially in a bad winter. By the end of February cuttings can be taken. Young shoots 2-4 in. (6-10 cm.) long can be taken and put in leaf-mould and sharp sand and covered with a pane of glass. Better still, use a plastic covering to prevent rot. When the cuttings are rooted, put them into pots filled with a mixutre of leaf-mould, fertilizer and sharp sand. Eventually put three cuttings together so as to have a well filled pot and do not forget the crocks at the bottom.

CRYPTANTHUS *Bromeliad*

These long-lasting Bromeliads are natives of the virgin forests of Brazil where they grow on trees and are, therefore, epiphytes.

On account of their beautifully striped and coloured leaves they are often used in decorative bowls. About a dozen species of this genus are known. They form rosettes like most of the Bromeliads, but the leaves are small and narrow so that the markings are more striking.

The stemless Bromeliads are the most useful in a room for they do not grow too tall nor do they need a moist atmosphere as the other kinds do. Since their root system is poorly developed, they can be put in small pots, in low bowls or, in their natural way, fastened to a tree trunk or a piece of cork. The more light they receive, the more intense will be the colour of the leaves, for Cryptanthus can stand the sun better than the other kinds. Only at mid-day in the summer, give them shade for an hour. In the winter they prefer a temperature not below 60°F (15°C) but a constant temperature of 65°F (18°C) is preferable. In winter the plant wants rather tepid water on the soil and in dry heat it can be sprayed with luke-warm water.

If it is fastened to the branch of a tree, then the ball of soil should be wrapped in moist sphagnum and thus kept damp with tepid water. The higher the plant hangs the quicker the moss will dry out because warm air rises and, therefore, the more often it should be sprayed.

Cryptanthus produces an insignificant inflorescence but it increases by means of offsets as many Bromeliads do. These develop at the base and when they are about half the length of the leaves of the mother plant, they should be removed. They root easily in damp sphagnum. They want a low pot or a bowl, three-quarters filled with crocks over which the sphagnum is spread and into which the young shoots will root. Give them water into the leaf rosette, using rain water for preference. Covering the pot with glass or plastic assists the rooting. Under a plastic cover, water the plants and then wait for three weeks before inspecting them; water and remove the cover to see if new growth has begun. Under glass the soil dries out more quickly and so water must be given sooner, preferably in the morning, otherwise the soil will dry out.

Although few roots have developed in the sphagnum, the new growth should be put into a small pot or a bowl with plenty of crocks at the bottom, in a mixture of leaf-mould, sphagnum, a little loam and sharp sand.

In the illustration: above, from left to right *Cryptanthus bromelioides tricolor*, *C. bromelioides*, *C. lubbersianus*. In the centre *C. bivittatus*. Below *C. zonatus zebrinus* and *C. fosterianus*.

CYCLAMEN

Although the Cyclamen is one of the best known indoor plants, there is often some uncertainty as to the treatment it requires. Sometimes the leaves hang down over the edge of the pot, or they may turn yellow, or perhaps the flower or leaf-stalks will rot just above the corm or the flower buds dry up. Light and air are the main factors for good cultivation and, above all, never put the plant in front of a stove. A temperature of 50°F (10°C) is really the most ideal for a flowering Cyclamen. The pot should be put as near the window as possible, in a low bowl so that it can be watered from below. The temperature of this water should be on the warm side and any that has not been absorbed in an hour, should be emptied out. The pot should not stand in water permanently or the leaves may turn yellow. If watered from above the corm may rot but, where there is central heating, however, it may be necessary to water on top as well.

If the leaves droop, this may be a sign of dryness, then soak the pot in a pail of tepid water until it ceases to bubble. Dead flowers should be removed, and fertilizer given weekly. When the plant has finished flowering it is often thrown away but it can be kept quite easily until the following spring by reducing the water supply, stopping the feeding and putting the plant in an unheated room. The old leaves will die off but as soon as new leaves appear, give it more water.

In May put it out of doors, if possible, in the shade or semi-shade, but first repot it in a mixture of 2 parts leaf-mould, 2 parts loam, 1 part peat and some sharp sand. The upper side of the corm should not be covered with soil. Until October it can be left out of doors and then gradually it should be accustomed to a higher temperature, about 50-60°F (10-15°C) to prevent the flower buds drying up.

On young leaves greenfly may develop which is removed by spraying with a mixture of methylated spirit, soft soap and water. Repeat if necessary.

CYPERUS DIFFUSUS *Umbrella Plant*

There is hardly a plant more aptly named than the Umbrella plant, for the shape can be likened to nothing better and, moreover, it wants a lot of water. The plant illustrated has rather broader leaves than the well-known *Cyperus alternifolius*. It often happens that amateurs spoil their plants by overwatering, but a Cyperus will soak up any amount and is therefore an ideal plant for the amateur.

It comes from the swamps of Madagascar, which explains its love of water, for it can even stand being continuously wet so that it can be stood in a bowl of water which is regularly filled up. If it gets too little water it will undoubtedly die.

It is one of the easiest plants to grow indoors provided it is in a hot or even a moderately warm room at about 50-55°F (10-13°C). It prefers not to be in the mid-day sun and does well in a room facing north or north-east. If the leaves turn yellowish brown in a dry atmosphere, put the plant out in the rain or spray it.

Withered tips should be cut off, leaving a short piece, otherwise the wound formed will go brown. It is advisable to keep the plant in good form by giving it weekly a dose of fertilizer which will produce a healthy plant with firm stems and fresh green leaves. Between the pointed leaves, small flowers may develop which, though not showy, are attractive on account of their brown colouring.

The plant can be propagated by detaching a leaf-rosette with about 1½-2 in. (3-4 cm) of stem, and trimming the leaves to a third of their length. It is then potted in damp soil consisting of equal parts of leaf-mould, loam and sharp sand and putting it under a glass or plastic cover. In a short time buds will appear in the axils of the leaves which develop into 'umbrellas' which quickly form roots. The cutting can also be rooted in a bowl of water and the stem can be bent back into the water so that young plants will develop more quickly. The plant can also be increased by dividing the root-stock.

CYTISUS RACEMOSUS *Broom*

In the spring, about Easter, there appears in the florist's shops a little evergreen shrub about 1½ ft. (40 cm) high, with little, short-stalked leaves and trusses of butter-yellow flowers. This is *Cytisus racemosus,* one of the Brooms, and belongs to the *Papilionaceae,* being a small relation of the *Laburnum;* it comes from the Canary Islands.

This Broom is generally in flower when acquired but it is possible that the flowers will not last long in the hot, dry air of a warm room. It dries up or collapses. Therefore give it a very bright, sunny position in a cool room that is unheated. A temperature of 45-55°F (8-12°C) is suitable. From March onwards it should be shaded from the mid-day sun, and kept moist regularly. Whilst in flower give it fertilizer every fortnight.

After flowering, cut the plant down to half its height to make it grow bushy. At the same time repot it in a rich but lime-free soil, using a pot two to three times larger, with crocks at the bottom. Good results can be obtained from 3 parts leaf-mould, 2 parts fertilizer and 1 part sharp sand. Some of the branches that have been cut off, 2-4 in. (6-10 cm) long can be used as cuttings. For preference take them with a heel, that is, with a part of the main stem. First dip them in water and then into a pot of leaf-mould and sharp sand at a temperature of 55-60°F (12-15°C). Cover them with paper if they are in a sunny place. Keep the soil moist but not too wet. By August or September the cuttings should have rooted. The mother plant can be left out of doors during the summer in a sheltered, sunny position where it should be sprayed if dry and given fertilizer once a fortnight. The pot should be turned round every three weeks to keep the plant in shape.

At the end of September or beginning of October, bring the plant back into the house and put it in an unheated room in the sun. It does not like artificial heat and a temperature of 45°F (8°C) is sufficient. In February or March it can be given a warmer position, 55-65°F (12-18°C) when the flowers should begin to appear.

DIEFFENBACHIA

Not so long ago this plant, with its beautifully marked leaves, was grown only in hot houses but now, owing to the better heating of our dwelling houses, it is offered in the trade as an indoor plant. In plant groups, especially where colour is needed, this tropical foliage plant is most often used. In the house *Dieffenbachia picta* and its hybrid *D. bausei* are the best. Natives of Brazil, these plants, which are related to the Arums, are accustomed to moist warmth and protection from the sun. They seldom flower in a room and the inflorescence is more curious than beautiful. The flower spike is partially enclosed in the greenish sheath and, to the eye, not very attractive. It is not essential to grow Dieffenbachias on the window sill; they will do well in a position further into the room. However, they do not want to be too far from the light or the beauty of the colouring may be spoilt. In spring and summer the plants want a lot of water, at room temperature, on the soil; rain water should be used if possible. So that the large leaves do not dry up in a hot room, they should be sponged daily or several times a week, depending on the atmosphere in the room. In winter the soil may be kept on the dry side and only watered if it is light in colour and feels dry.

Spraying the leaves is, however, as important in winter as in summer, but water should not be allowed to stand in the saucer. From March to October Dieffenbachias need fertilizer every fortnight. In winter the temperature should not fall below 60 °F (15 °C) and, for this foliage plant, 65-70 °F (18-20°C) is preferable. The moist atmosphere can be provided, during the period when the stove is on, by putting a kettle of water on the stove and saucers of water on a special damper on the radiator. The pot can also be stood on a low support in a bowl of water, but the water should not reach the pot itself, or damp sphagnum can be packed between the pot and the decorative pot in which it stands, to increase the humidity of the air.

When it outgrows its pot, then in March it can be put into another, one or two sizes larger, with a layer of crocks at the bottom. A loose but nourishing mixture should be used, for example, 3 parts leaf mould, 1 part loam or fine clay, 1 part fertilizer and some peat. Dieffenbachias can be propagated by cuttings and by means of stems that have become bare, about 2 in. (5 cm) long. The sap is poisonous! Let them dry and stand them erect in sharp sand at a high temperature 70-75°F (20-25°C) under a sheet of glass or plastic. In a room the cuttings will generally root successfully.

DIPLADENIA

A climbing plant from South America, this is one of the newer indoor plants. There is the white *Dipladenia boliviensis* with funnel-shaped flowers with yellow centres, and the pink *D. sanderi rosea* with larger flowers which, in spring and summer, are used as house plants. The buds form on shoots that are one year old. The white species has a delicious fragrance.

Anyone who has acquired a young plant which is not yet beginning to climb should, if the nurseryman has not already done so, give it some support. It wants plenty of light (do not put it behind a curtain) and can tolerate full sun but, in summer, shade it during the middle of the day. Always use tepid water and then let it dry out as the roots are rather sensitive. All through the year, the leaves should be sprayed with tepid water daily, for it dislikes a dry atmosphere. During the winter very little water is needed on the soil. In spring and summer, while the buds are forming, Dipladenias want fertilizer every fortnight. In the winter they are rested. Keep them in a warm room, as bright and sunny as possible, where the temperature does not fall below 60°F (15°C).

To make it flower well, it is advisable to shorten the stems in February or March. If it has outgrown its pot, it can be repotted at the same time, using one that is one or two sizes larger. A rich but open soil is advisable, such as a mixture of woodland soil, fertilizer, fine clay, peat dust and sharp sand. Since the roots are rather sensitive, the drainage must be adequate and a good layer of crocks put at the bottom of the pot. Thereafter, keep the pot in a warm place.

Tips cut off, about 3-4 in. (6-10 cm) long, with the lowest leaves removed, and even longer stems, can be rooted. They can be put separately into small pots or several together into a larger one, in which case they are planted round the edge and, in this way, root more quickly. A suitable soil for cuttings is leaf-mould or loam with sharp sand. They can be put under a plastic cover. Give them a light warm place but not in the sun. After three weeks, water when necesary and remove the cover. Gradually accustom them to the warmth of the room and repot them into a soil mixture given above.

These plants are susceptible to mealy bug, scale insects and red spider. White bits of fluff or brown, oval scales, if they appear, can be dabbed with methylated spirit; this can be repeated in 10 or 14 days, and again if necessary.

DRACAENA *Dragon Tree*

These foliage plants, which are found in Tropical Asia and Africa, are now-a-days much used for decoration in the house. Several kinds are shown in the illustration. From left to right *Dracaena bruantii* (*Cordyline rubra* 'Bruantii'), *D. volckartii, D. massangeana.* In the centre *Dracaena godseffiana,* in the foreground *D. marginata* and *D. sanderiana.* Dracaenas may produce scented, lily like flowers but this rarely happens in a room. The common name of Dragon Tree (or sometimes Dragon's Blood Tree) is due to the fact that, when damaged, it exudes a red, resinous liquid.
The plant wants a temperature of 65-70°F (18-20°C) which in winter or at night should not fall below 55°F (12°C). It likes plenty of light but from March to September should not be in the mid-day sun. It does not like draughts. In the winter is wants tepid water on the soil and the leaves should be sponged once a week. Depending on the more or less dry warmth, the plant should be sprayed with tepid water about once a week.
Between March and October a Dracaena wants fertilizer once a fortnight. In the summer it needs more water and now and then to be put out in the rain. Loosening the surface of the soil is recommended.
Repotting every year is not necessary and should only be done when the roots are coming through the bottom of the pot. For preference repotting should be done late in the spring, about the end of April or beginning of May, into a pot one or two sizes larger. A crock with the rounded side upwards is placed over the hole and then a layer of sharp sand to prevent the roots rotting. Fill up with a mixture of leaf-mould, fertilizer, loam and sharp sand.
Sometimes there is a complaint that a Dracaena in a room loses its lowest leaves. Usually this can be avoided by spraying occasionally in the winter or by putting the plant further from the stove or radiators. Plants whose stems have become bare can be divided up and treated as cuttings; they should be stood erect in sharp sand and placed under a glass or plastic cover. The leafy tops with about 6 leaves can be cut off and will produce new plants. February or March is a good time to take cuttings and they will need to be kept at a temperature of 70°F (20°C) at least. If the old plant is cut down to about 4 in. (10 cm) high, it will form side shoots.
The dry, warm air makes them susceptible to scale and red spider which should be removed by spraying with methylated spirit. Spray the under sides of the leaves also and repeat in 8-10 days.

ECHEVERIA SETOSA

The Echeverias, which come from Mexico, are succulent plants which are easy to grow. Among the 150 and more species belonging to this genus there are many which are grown solely for the leaf rosette but there are others which will flower and are, in fact, so floriferous that even people who do not like succulent plants will like them.

A low-growing species is *Echeveria setosa* with hairy leaves in a close rosette and many-flowered spikes about June, closely covered with red and yellow, bell-shaped flowers, red at the base and yellow at the edge. When in bloom the whole plant is not more than 4-6 in. (10-15 cm) high. The small leaves, which are arranged round the stems, fall off at the slightest touch and scatter so that one should not be surprised to find that, in a near-by pot, young Echeverias are developing, which may flower in a year's time.

The treatment is simple; put the plant in a light position, in front of a window, in the sun if possible, and it should not be given too much water. The more light it gets, the more compact the rosette will remain and, for this reason, do not put it behind a curtain. Give plenty of fresh air in the summer or plant out of doors in a dry, sunny position. In the winter the plant likes a temperature of 45-50°F (6-10°C) but preferably not near a stove, and water sparingly. Completely dry is best but it is possible then that the leaves would dry up.

When the plant needs repotting, which should be done after flowering, use a mixture of leaf-mould, charcoal, sharp sand and crushed mortar rubble, in which it grows best.

The leaves of the rosette, like the rosette itself, can be used for propagating. Break off and leave to dry for several hours, then put them into leaf-mould and sharp sand during the spring and summer.

Echeveria setosa is one of the Echeverias that flower in summer like *E. pilosa* and *E. peacockii*.

The ones that flower in winter are *Echeveria carnicolor, E. retusa* and *E. acutifolia;* the latter is better known as *E. gibbiflora metallica,* conspicuous with its large rosettes which are violet pink with a bronze sheen. The long, leafy flower stems carry little bright pink flowers.

EPIPHYLLUM HYBRIDUM *Phyllocactus*

As spring approaches, about the middle of January or beginning of February, Phyllocacti may be brought out of the cooler room where they have been resting during the winter. On the edges of the flattened stems, for Phyllocactus has flattened stems that look like leaves, little buds appear from which, in the warmth of a living room, will develop enormous flowers in various shades of red, pink, orange, yellow and white, according to the variety.

The Phyllocacti come from Mexico and Central America and are used to a cool, dry climate and need a cool sunny environment here in the winter at a temperature of 45-50°F (6-10° C) when they need little water. The resting period lasts from November to the middle of January or beginning of February.

During the resting period the buds are formed which later will develop into flowers in a warmer place, provided the plant is not turned round, for the buds always face the light.

After flowering it is best not to put the plant in the mid-day sun since the growing period now begins and then a sunless window or one that only gets sun in the morning is better; give plenty of water and spray the crown; once a fortnight give it fertilizer to encourage growth. Eventually the plant can be put out of doors in the summer months in a shady place. If the shoots get too long, in late summer the tops can be cut off, which encourages the formation of buds.

Cuttings can easily be taken and a good soil mixture for them is leaf-mould, loam and sharp sand. It is not necessary to use only the tips; other parts of the stem, about 3-4 in. (6-10 cm) long can also be rooted. The base should be cut wedge-shaped, close to the areoles and from there obliquely upwards to the centre. The cuttings should first be left to dry for a week or two before being put into soil. Be careful that the upper end is at the top. Cover the lower areoles (growing points) with soil. The small pot containing the cuttings is put inside a larger one filled with granulated peat which is kept moist, so that they will not rot off. A glass or plastic cover is placed over the small pot as this encourages rooting. Later repot into leaf-mould, fertilizer, loam and sharp sand and, if possible, clay or loam.

Cuttings which are put in the soil upside down will not root. By making an oblique cut, the chance of rooting is increased. No round stems will root.

ERICA *Heath*

Where else should we look for heaths than in the country when on holiday, but we do not expect to find them in living rooms except, perhaps, cut branches brought home as a souvenir. That kind of heath would not be a success as an indoor plant. But nurserymen have introduced several kinds of Erica which, with a little care, will last in the house for a considerable time.
Erica gracilis or Slender Heath, shown in the illustration, flowers in November and December, with pyramidal trusses of purple-red flowers which remind us of our shrubby heath. It is a graceful plant which will flower for several months in a fairly warm or unheated but frost-free room.
Coming originally from South Africa, this Heath has been in cultivation in Germany and England for a very long time and it is therefore remarkable that is was first introduced to Holland in the spring of 1934.
Give it plenty of light but not too much sun, rain water for preference and fertilizer every fortnight. After flowering it is difficult to keep in the house, although it might do in front of an open window in the morning sun. Putting it in a greenhouse will not be successful, nor putting it in full sun, nor under the drip of trees or shrubs; a dying plant should be thrown away in any case, for it is hopeless to try and save it.
Erica gracilis is followed by *Erica hiemalis* or Winter Heath, which flowers profusely and may be reckoned among the most beautiful of the winter-flowering plants. *Erica persoluta* covers itself with white flowers from March to May. In early summer another Erica appears in the florist's shops, *Erica ventricosa,* which has pink, tubular flowers somewhat swollen at the base, which appear in September. This is rather difficult to keep but success is more likely in an unheated room. Do not forget to water it or the leaves will fall, but be careful that the soil is not too moist. It is much better to spray over the plants. Above all, this plant prefers heath soil mixed with sharp sand and peat, in any case it wants a very poor soil.
The garden plant, *Erica carnea,* Winter Heath, which flowers from January to April, and *Erica vagans* from July to September, can also be used as pot plants and will last in bloom for a long time.
All Ericas can be increased by cuttings in August and September. Cuttings about 3-4 in. (6-10 cm) long should be put in a box or pot of peat and covered with glass.

EUPHORBIA FULGENS *E. jacquiniiflora*

The various kinds of Euphorbia belong to the Spurge family; some of them are succulent but this one is not particularly so.

Euphorbia fulgens, also known as *E. jacquiniiflora,* is a most attractive shrub with narrow, pointed leaves on graceful, arching stems; the flowers arise from the axils of the leaves and are inconspicuous but are surrounded by bright, orange bracts. This Euphorbia is all too rarely met with as an indoor plant, although it is one of the most satisfactory of the winter flowering kinds as, from November to February, it bears its attractive pseudoflowers. It must be given a very light place and plenty of water but the plant should be moved as little as possible. After flowering, when the resting time begins, it is kept completely dry in the corner of a warm room. In April, after the resting period, remove the old soil and re-pot in sandy soil, not too rich, but with the addition of leaf-mould, fertilizer and a little clay; above all, do not use too large a pot, but put plenty of crocks at the bottom.

To keep the plant low and compact it is advisable to cut it down after the resting period. Wounds should be covered with powdered charcoal or white sand. After trimming and repotting the plant, put it in a sunny room, at a temperature of 65-70°F (15-20°C). At first give a moderate amount of water but, as growth begins, give it fertilizer every fortnight. At the end of May and beginning of June, put it in a sunny but sheltered place out of doors and bring it in again in September. If it remains in the house give it plenty of fresh air.

Should there be any doubt as to whether a plant is an Euphorbia or not, prick the stem and, if a drop of white juice appears, that will settle the question. When a branch is cut off a Euphorbia the milky liquid or latex at once runs out and the plant may slowly bleed to death. The cut end should immediately be put into the flame of a lighted candle or into hot water 4-6 in. (10-15 cm) deep for about a minute. Then put the flowering stems into a vase of tepid water where they will last for several weeks.

Cuttings can be taken between March and July, the ends dipped in powdered charcoal which should also be rubbed into the cut on the mother plant. Use peat and sharp sand in the pot into which the cuttings are to be rooted and stand it on a warm surface or keep it at a temperature of 70°F (20°C). Cover it with glass or plastic; it will need no water for three weeks under plastic, then give it water as required.

EUPHORBIA MILLII *Crown of Thorns*

Most of the Euphorbias, such as *E.pulcherrima (Poinsettia)* and *E.fulgens,* which are also used as house plants, are not so easy to keep as *Euphorbia milii (E.splendens)* which is popularly known as the Crown of Thorns. The long, branching stems are covered with long, pointed, dark brown thorns whilst the small, light green leaves grow mainly towards the tips. The flowers develop between the new leaves, and the flower stalks are sticky and have bright red bracts. Most Euphorbias are more showy when in flower but do not last long. *Euphorbia millii,* however, remains in flower for months and, in fact, is seldom without flowers. The plant comes from Madagascar where it occurs in the mountains, which means that it can stand heat as well as cooler conditions. However, it does like a sunny position and it seldom needs shading. Only in the middle of summer it prefers the morning sun and plenty of fresh air. It can be planted out of doors from June to September in a sunny, sheltered place.

If cuttings are required, young shoots about 3-4 in. (6-10 cm) long should be taken and after leaving them to dry for a few hours put them into a pot with sandy soil where they will root quickly and even produce a few flowers the first year. They root more quickly if dipped in.

When taking the cuttings it is important not to lose too much sap and therefore the lower end of the cutting and the wound on the mother plant must be treated with powdered charcoal or white sand. Be careful of touching wounds, for the sap is poisonous.

A good soil mixture for Euphorbias is 1 part of garden loam, a quarter part of sharp sand or equal parts of leaf-mould and loam with some sharp sand added. In summer give plenty of water and spray the plant on warm days, and once a fortnight give fertilizer, but during the winter take care there is not too much moisture in the atmosphere; this plant would do well in the dry air of a living room. Never water when the soil is wet and still dark in colour and feels damp and do not feed it at all until new growth begins. The chance of the leaves dropping off is small at a temperature of 60°F (15°C). When it gets too big it can be pruned to any shape and the wounds should be protected as described for cuttings.

Usually this plant is better known by florists under the name *Euphorbia splendens.*

EUPHORBIA PULCHERRIMA *Poinsettia*

It is hardly necessary to describe this plant for, at Christmas time, almost all florists display this Poinsettia, together with the Christmas Rose, either as a cut flower or as a pot plant. If a plant is received as a present at Christmas, put it in a light position in a warm room, preferably in a south window where it will not have to be moved; give it plenty of water and spray the leaves. Shifting the plant about may spoil it, for it is one of the Euphorbias or Spurges, and care must be taken because the slightest injury will cause the poisonous, milky sap to run out.

It may not be generally realised that the beautiful red leaves are not the real flowers, but bracts surrounding the tiny, inconspicuous flowers in the centre. When the bracts fall, no more water should be given. The plant will now lose all its leaves and should be cut down to 3-4 in. (7-10 cm), treating the wound with powdered charcoal, and then kept completely dry in a room where it will not be in a very bright place and the temperature not too low. In April the old soil should be carefully shaken off and the plant repotted in a mixture of equal parts of leaf-mould, clay and fertilizer. Then put it back in its original place in a warm room in a south window and give it only a little water at first, but as the plant begins to grow, water it more often. When it is growing well this plant needs feeding, so give it fertilizer weekly or fortnightly. By the middle of June it can be put out in the garden, plunged in a sunny, sheltered place where it can be sprayed if dry and given fertilizer once a fortnight. In September bring it in again and put it in its old position at a temperature of 70° F (20°C), where it should be sprayed overhead daily and given fertilizer regularly. By the beginning of December a temperature of 60°F (15°C) is sufficient.

If a flowering branch is to be cut off, then the lower part of the stem should either be burned or dipped into hot water for one minute, then into tepid water containing preservative.

EXACUM AFFINE

A small plant which, in summer and autumn, bears little lilac blue flowers with yellow centres which resemble those of the potato. But Exacum is not related for it belongs to the Gentian familly and comes from South-East Asia.

The one most often grown is *Exacum affine atrocoeruleum,* whose flowers are darker in colour. It is generally grown as an annual, but it can be increased by cuttings. Sow it in a warm room in a mixture of leaf-mould and sharp sand, the upper 1 in. (3 cm) of soil should be sieved. The seed should be covered with soil to its own depth. Press it down and spray to keep it moist. Cover it with a sheet of glass, which should be wiped daily to remove the moisture that has condensed on it.

When the plants are large enough to handle, put them three together into pots 4-4½ in. (10-12 cm) in diameter. The soil mixture should be 3 parts leaf-mould, 2 parts fertilizer and 1 part loam, with peat at the bottom.

After repotting, keep them cooler and shade from the sun. Exacum does very well in a window where it gets no sun.

The flowers appear about six months after sowing, that is, about the end of July or the beginning of August. Give a fair amount of water whilst it is growing and flowering, and fertilizer every fortnight until no more buds are formed. It wants plenty of fresh air in summer and eventually single plants can be put out of doors in the shade.

If the leaves have not dried up or fallen off, it can be put in a fairly warm, light room, but only give enough water for the leaves to remain fresh, and no fertilizer.

About February or March, cuttings can be taken, about 2½-4 in. (6-10 cm) long, and put in a pot of leaf mould and sharp sand. Five cuttings round the edge of the pot should root easily, then put them into separate pots and treat them as given above for seedlings.

Put in a warm room under glass or plastic covers and shade from the sun. Under plastic they need no water for three weeks, until they begin to grow. Then gradually remove the covers to prevent them becoming drawn.

FATSHEDERA LIZEI

An attractive modern plant which, unfortunately, has no common name by which it can be called. That it is a cross between *Fatsia* and the Ivy *(Hedera helix)* is a fact easier to remember than the Latin name. In appearance it is stiffer than *Fatsia* since the leaf stalks are not so long and the stem rarely branches but it usually grows fairly tall. The leaf itself is smaller and it has adapted itself to the climbing habit of the Ivy so that it can easily cover a wall. Three plants are generally put together in one pot so as to get a more compact and bushy effect. Besides the usual green form there is one with variegated leaves which needs more light and heat.

On the whole Fatshedera is an easy plant to grow indoors, suitable for a sunless room or hall, and need not be put in the window. In summer it may be planted outside in semi-shade but it is not hardy in winter like *Fatsia* and Ivy and so must be brought in at the beginning of October. If it is to remain in the house, during the summer give it plenty of air and stand the pot out in the rain when possible. It needs plenty of water and fertilizer every fortnight is advisable; the leaves should be sponged weekly. Little water and no feeding are required during the winter months.

When the plant gets too tall, the top can be layered, as described for *Fatsia japonica.* The rest of the stem can be cut into pieces, each having two leaves. Remove the lowest of these leaves and plant three pieces together in leaf-mould and sharp sand. Keep them moist and cover with a pane of glass or a bell jar, putting them in a warm place but not in direct sunlight. If about 8 inches of the original stem is left, it will start growing again and make a bushy plant.

In a very dry atmosphere red spider may appear, recognised by the brown coloration of the leaf and on the undersides a web. This should be sprayed with insecticide. After 10-14 days repeat if necessary.

FATSIA JAPONICA

Fatsia is one of the fastest growing of the larger indoor plants. The leaves are shaped like a hand, long-stalked, rather leathery and light green in colour; there is also a variegated form, *Fatsia japonica variegata,* which is not so strong.

To keep this plant in good condition, give it a cool place both in summer and winter, since direct sunlight or even a warm, dry atmosphere will make the leaves turn yellow. A room facing north, north-east or north-west gives the best results; in summer it wants plenty of water and fertilizer every fortnight, whilst it will benefit by being put out in the rain occasionally.

In winter a temperature of 40°F (4°C) is sufficient. It wants only a little water which, if possible, should have the chill off, and feeding should be stopped. All through the year the plant should be sponged once a week to remove the dust and discourage pests. If water is left in the saucer under the pot, the plant will lose its lower leaves.

In summer it may be planted out in the garden in semi-shade and, when it gets too large for the room it can be treated as a garden shrub. In that case, take it out of its pot and plant it in a sheltered corner where it will grow into a large bush and may even flower.

The objection to a Fatsia in the house is that the stem becomes bare at the base and this can be remedied by layering, a form of propagation where an upward cut about 1½-2 in. (3-4 cm) long is made in the stem going only so far as the centre. The cut must be kept open by inserting a piece of wood or small stone. A wad of damp moss is tied round and kept moist; into this the new roots will grow; if plastic material is bound round, it will prevent the moss drying out. During the process the plant itself should not be watered so that most of the food will collect about the cut and root formation is thereby encouraged. As soon as the roots come through the moss, the top of the plant, which is now rooted, should be cut off. The moss is removed and the new plant repotted in good soil. Do not forget the crocks at the bottom of the pot.

FICUS ELASTICA *Rubber Plant*

An old fashioned foliage plant which is now seen again in modern settings is *Ficus elastica,* Young specimens are the most attractive on account of their leathery leaves which are suffused with a bronzy sheen, whilst the top-most leaf is still enveloped in a reddish sheath, the colour being more pronounced if it is in the sun. The variegated form is called *Ficus elastica variegata.*

Since Ficus grows slowly, it will give pleasure for years. Repot it every two to three years, in equal parts of leaf-mould and well-rotted manure or fertilizer and sharp sand. If it becomes too large, the top can be cut off and used as a cutting, or the plant layered. (See Fatsia). If the top is still not woody, it can be treated as a cutting and the best result is usually obtained if the cut is made below the top three or four leaves. Cover the cut surface immediately with powdered charcoal or white sand, to prevent the sap running out. Ficus loves sunshine, particularly in winter and spring, and is then at its best provided it is given plenty of water and fertilizer every fortnight. Anyone who has a garden should put the plant out from June to September, where it can be treated in the same way. If it remains in the house, then shade it from the midday sun. Sponge the leaves once a week.

In winter it does not want direct heat; all that is required is that it should not be put in a place where the temperature at night falls below 50°F (10°C) and where it will get the sun as early as possible. Avoid draughts or considerable changes of temperature between night and day. Give it a moderate amount of water at room temperature but only when the soil is light coloured and dry.

When cuttings are taken of a Ficus, the cut stems which should have at least two leaves, are put in a flask of water in the sun to encourage rooting; as soon as the roots appear, the cuttings are put into a pot with good soil, kept in the shade and covered with glass, or in a plastic bag to prevent them drying out. To make the plant branch, take out the top or cut a circular ring through the bark directly under a leaf. By coagulation of the sap, food collects above the cut and a dormant bud begins to develop.

The plant is susceptible to red spider, recognisable by the brown colouring and the web on the underside of the leaves. Spray with an insecticide and repeat in 10-14 days. Do not forget to spray the underside. Sunken yellow patches with black edges indicate leaf spot disease. Prevent this spreading by spraying with a solution of copper carbonate in water.

FICUS PUMILA *Ficus repens*

A dwarf relation of the fig and of the better known Rubber Plant, *Ficus elastica,* it is a native of Japan and China. Nurserymen know it as *Ficus pumila minima,* small-leaved.

It is one of the most popular climbing plants or hanging plants for modern interiors and grows quickly when conditions suit it. The long, graceful branches are self-attaching and bear small, kidney-shaped leaves set obliquely to the stem.

This Ficus is very accomodating and will grow anywhere. It grows equally in a warm or a cool room, in full sun or where the light is poor. Therefore it is suitable for corners where few other plants would like to live and also is useful for framing the doors of a room. It does not like full sun but grows better in a bright than in a dark position but since rapid growers are not wanted as wall covering, the slower growth does not matter.

In summer give it plenty of water, if the atmosphere of the room is warm and dry; spray the plant well overhead or put it out in the rain. In spring and summer give fertilizer every fortnight. In winter it does not want feeding and should be given less water; the amount depends on the temperature of its surroundings. In a hot room spraying is necessary to prevent the leaves curling.

There is also a variegated form, *Ficus pumila minima variegata,* the leaves of which are smaller but, like all variegated plants, it requires more light and cannot stand the cold so well.

There is also *Ficus rubiginosa (australis) variegata,* a sturdy indoor plant with oval variegated leaves and a bushy habit of growth. It does well on a window sill out of the sun and requires the same treatment as *Ficus pumila.* It shows no tendency to climb.

For the treatment of red spider see under *Ficus elastica.*

FUCHSIA

There are only a few plants which lend themselves to all purposes and they are all worth growing, especially the old-fashioned Fuchsia, which can be treated entirely as an outdoor subject, put out on the balcony or used for bedding out in the garden.

Obviously for these different purposes, different varieties are required. What then is the treatment required for the Fuchsia which can be left in a room continuously all the year round? It wants a position with plenty of light and where it will get the morning sun, and it must be kept moist in the summer and be sprayed now and then. The flowers are inclined to drop easily, therefore do not move the plant more than necessary, nor turn it round. For choice it should be put beside a window that is kept open. If given fertilizer every fortnight, the plant will keep its flowers much longer.

A plant that is put out in the summer in semi-shade wants the same sort of treatment. At the end of September or beginning of October, it is brought in again and overwintered in a cool room or a greenhouse. During the resting period very little water is needed and no feeding. In February bring it into a warm place, trim the plant and give it fertilizer as soon as new growth appears.

In the spring it is advisable, at the same time as it is cut back, to give it fresh soil such as loam or compost with leaf-mould and fertilizer; the pot should be covered with glass or plastic to provide a moist atmosphere. July and August is also a good time to take cuttings; they will root in a bottle of water in a sunny room.

White fly, which often attacks Fuchsias, can be dealt with by spraying with D.D.T. Repeat after 3 days. Greenfly can be removed by spraying with soft soap and methylated spirit; repeat when necessary.

GARDENIA JASMINOIDES *Cape Jasmine*

In the previous century, the pure white, sweet scented Gardenia was the favourite flower for corsage or buttonhole but the plant itself was scarcely known to its admirers. Now that it can be purchased in florist's shops it has become popular.

Gardenia jasminoides, also known as *Gardenia florida,* comes from China and is an evergreen shrub, with shining, light green, ovate or lanceolate leaves. The large, flat, white flowers remind one of a *Camellia.* But a Gardenia when well grown may produce flower buds throughout the year, though the usual flowering period is from May until the beginning of August and is sometimes prolonged into October and November.

A Gardenia makes very attractive buds but it is an art to make them all develop. The trouble usually is that many of the buds drop off; this is annoying but can be avoided by shading the plant as much as possible from too much light and making sure that the night temperature does not fall below 60-65°F (16-18°C). In a dull, wet summer this phenomenon often occurs.

Besides plenty of light, a Gardenia will stand full sun, especially in the summer months, provided it is shaded from the mid-day sun for some hours. In summer it wants plenty of water on the soil, which should not be cold. Moreover the plant dislikes lime so rain water should be used. Do not forget to water it or the buds may fall off.

The regular spraying of the leaves and buds provides a moist atmosphere, an important factor for success. Later, whilst it is growing and flowering, give fertilizer occasionally. In winter, a definite rest is essential, so that the possibility of the formation of new buds is not hindered. Spraying the leaves and buds regularly to maintain a moist atmosphere is also a factor for its success. Give water in moderation, tepid for choice.

After flowering the plant should be pruned. If necessary, repot it in the spring in soil free from lime but containing humus, for example, woodland soil or leaf-mould with clay and sharp sand. Cut off the tips 3-4 in. (7-10 cm) long, put them ¾ in. (2 cm) deep into pots with leaf-mould and sharp sand under a plastic cover. The plastic is removed gradually as new growth appears so that it may grow freely. Spray it well and remove one or two of the tips to encourage growth. A temperature above 65°F (18°C) gives the best chance of success.

It is probable that it will produce buds in the second year.

GESNERIA *Corytholoma*

The correct name for this plant is *Corytholoma* but it was introduced to commerce as *Gesneria,* especially the varieties *G. cardinalis* or *G. macrantha.* On account of its flaming red, pipe-shaped flowers it has been given several common names abroad.

Gesneria has a tuberous rhizome and is therefore easy to keep until the following year. It flowers in the summer months. Like the *Gloxinia* it prefers a position that is not too cool, plenty of light but not full sun. It wants plenty of water, preferably at room temperature, but the velvety leaves should not be allowed to get wet or brown stains may appear. Give it fertilizer once a fortnight and the flowers may last well into the spring.

When the plant begins to go off, reduce the watering and stop feeding; at the same time give it more sun, which makes the leaves die off more quickly, and stop watering altogether. Leave the tuber in the pot and keep it dry during the winter in a place that is not too cool, for example, in a cupboard where the temperature is not below 40°F (6°C).

In February or March, growth begins again and the tuber should be shaken free of the old soil and repotted in a mixture of coarse loam or leaf-mould, turf and fertilizer and sharp sand. The tubers should not be planted too deep, the soil only just covering them.

At first the tuber does not need light, only warmth, so put it on the mantlepiece or radiator, where it should be watered. Cover it with glass or plastic and spray the soil. When growth begins and green shoots appear, move the pot into full daylight in a warm room and give fertilizer once a fortnight. The young plants can be well sprayed so as to produce a moist atmosphere but, as soon as the buds appear, do not moisten the leaves any more. The greener it is in spring, the more it must be shaded from the mid-day sun. Young shoots may form in the autumn; in that case give plenty of water and keep the temperature above 55°F (12°C).

GLOXINIA *Sinningia*

One of the most popular plants for use indoors is *Gloxinia hybrida grandiflora,* with velvety, bell-shaped flowers, which is seen in the florist's as early as May and will still be there in August.

Gloxinia is a tuberous plant coming originally from Brazil, which had at first only blue flowers but later blue with a white edge, red and red with a white edge were produced.

Obviously the plant must be kept in flower as long as possible, so a favourable position should be found which must not be in the sun or the leaves will soon droop and there is a risk that the dreaded greenfly will attack it. Should it do so, spray with a mixture of soft soap, methylated spirit and water. It does, however, need a light, warm place, preferably at a temperature of 65-70°F (18-20°C) where it should be stood on an inverted saucer in a bowl of water which will be evaporating continuously. Use tepid water on the soil and give a dose of fertilizer once a week. This treatment is continued until the leaves wither and in the autumn the resting period begins. Reduce the watering until the leaves have died and then keep the plant quite dry during the winter, at a moderate temperature, not below 40°F (6°C), in a cupboard in a cool room. If kept too cold the tubers may rot.

In February or March start the dry tubers into growth in a bowl of peat in a warm place about 70°F (20-22°C), preferably under glass or plastic. Put the bowl on a warm mantlepiece or radiator. When the shoots are about 2 in. (4-5 cm) long, repot the tuber in a rich material such as leaf-mould, fertilizer and sharp sand. Retain three shoots and remove the rest. When in full growth again the same treatment can be followed and the leaves sprayed until the buds form. When the shoots are fully grown, the pot can be put in a light place but shaded from the mid-day sun; as far as possible, the temperature should be 65-70°F (18-20°C).

It is appreciated when the plant does not even lose its leaves in the autumn. In that case, keep the plant in a warm room and give it a moderate amount of tepid water.

GREVILLEA ROBUSTA *Silky Oak*

In the winter it is particularly pleasant to see green foliage in the house, and plants with attractive leaves are more sought after than in summer time. Such a foliage plant is *Grevillea robusta* which is seen all too seldom as an indoor plant. The leaf is very delicate and soft, somewhat resembling a Fern and the young leaves have a silvery sheen. Coming from a subtropical climate, Australia, it stands up well to the variations in the weather so that it can be put in the garden in the summer, in shade or semi-shade, provided it is brought in again at the latest at the beginning of October, according to the weather. In spring and summer it wants a lot of water and fertilizer every fortnight. But it is better to give it a little water every day rather than too much at one time. In winter it does not like too much heat and a temperature of 45-50°F (6-10°C) is sufficient, with little water and no feeding. Also the leaves should not be sprayed.

Grevillea is an attractive house plant and easy to please; it prefers a light place but not in full sun which tends to discolour the leaves. In a satisfactory position it is a quick grower and in three or four years may attain a considerable size. Where space is limited, its rapid growth will naturally be a drawback, but it can easily be grown from seed so that it can be started again and the old plant given away. In February or March sow in boxes under glass at a temperature of (18-20°C) 65°F. When they are large enough to handle the plants are put into small pots. Within a year the plants will be a fair size. The best soil mixture consists of garden soil, sieved loam, sand and fertilizer, a complicated mixture that is best made up by the nurseryman. Above all, do not forget to put crocks at the bottom.

To obtain a sturdy plant Grevillea should be repotted several times and the time when this should be done is obvious from the plant itself It does not flower until it has become a tree, a stage that will not be reached in indoor cultivation and therefore it is regarded as a foliage plant here.

GYNURA SARMENTOSA

Since plants have taken their place in our rooms, the need for coloured foliage plants to alternate with green ones is greater than ever.

To-day the new house plant, *Gynura sarmentosa,* with its beautiful violet hairs and velvety covering has spread very quickly. Moreover, this plant, which comes from India, is one of the easiest plants for a room and, though it likes more light and sun, it still keeps its beautiful colour.

Gynura is among the few indoor plants which can be grown in a sunny room the whole year through. Even in the height of summer, no shading is necessary. It can stand a temperature of 75-80°F (25-30°C), therefore it wants plenty of water in the soil in spring and summer and not too much fertilizer. Once a month is sufficient, otherwise it will grow too tall. Plenty of fresh air is required in summer.

In winter a temperature of 60-65°F (15-18°C) is suitable so long as it does not go below 55°F (12°C). From November to March it needs less water and fertilizer.

When necessary the plant can be trimmed at the beginning of March and the stem should eventually be tied to a stake. The plant will probably need repotting into a pot one or two sizes larger, in a mixture of 3 parts leaf-mould, 2 parts fertilizer and 1 part loam; put a crock at the bottom with the curved side uppermost. It grows well in the soil supplied by nurserymen, but add to this some fertilizer.

The tips that have been cut off, 3-4 in. (6-10 cm) long, can be used as cuttings, the lowest leaves being removed. They root easily in a flask of water in a sunny room. As soon as they have rooted, pot them up, one cutting in each pot, or three cuttings in a larger pot, which makes a bushier plant more quickly. One or two branches may be layered. In the course of the summer the orange flowers will appear, rather like a small Dandelion, for Gynura is also a member of the *Compositae.* The flower is not spectacular and moreover, flowering may cause the plant to lose it soft violet hairs; to prevent this, the flowers should be removed. An experiment can be tried; since the plant deteriorates after flowering, cuttings can be taken up to the end of October. The young plants usually have the best colours.

HEDERA HELIX *Ivy*

Just as in the garden the Ivy is an indestructable plant, so also in the house it is one of the sturdiest of climbing or hanging plants. The most beautiful green variety is 'Pittsburg', a small-leaved, narrowly pointed Ivy which is easily trained along a wall and can be used as a hanging plant on the corner of a bookcase or the piano.

Indoors as well as out, the Ivy makes no special demands but the colour of the leaves will be more beautiful if not exposed to full sun. Naturally it is better in a good light but it does quite well in a dark corner of the room and then should not be kept too warm. For a sunless room the Ivy is the ideal plant.

Give it plenty of water in the summer and occasionally stand it out in the rain. Give it fertilizer once a fortnight. In the winter, put it in an atmosphere that is not too dry and in a fairly cool place; water sparingly but do not feed. In spring and summer the tips 3-4 in. (about 6-10 cm) long may be nipped out, treated as cuttings and potted up in good garden soil. They will also root in a flask of water and when they have rooted, put them in a small pot with crocks at the bottom and a mixture of loam, leaf-mould and fertilizer. The plant illustrated on the left is *Hedera canariensis* 'Gloire de Marengo', distinguished by its larger leaves with creamy white markings; this variety has the leaves much more deeply divided and is sometimes not recognised as an Ivy.

It is less sturdy than the green Ivy and needs more light to preserve the beauty of the markings, and in winter wants a warmer, moister position. Sponge the leaves weekly for the edges quickly dry up and sometimes pests attack them. Scale insects can be dealt with by removing the scales and spraying with methylated spirit and the following day spray with soft soap or a nicotine preparation. And thrips (a silvery coloration with small black stripes) which should be treated with D.D.T. or a mixture of soft soap, methylated spirit, nicotine and water. After 10-14 days repeat if necessary. Yellow or brown patches with a web on the underside of the leaf suggests red spider, which should be sprayed with insecticide. Repeat if necessary.

HELLEBORUS NIGER *Christmas Rose*

Although it seems exaggerated to say that Christmas is not Christmas without the Christmas Rose, yet the white flowers amongst all the reds of Christmas decoration seem to bring us something of the spirit of Christmastide; they can be used mixed with other flowers or in a vase alone. This winter-flowering plant is indeed remarkable for, when all nature is asleep, it grows most vigorously and even in bitter cold weather, produces a lovely show of flowers.

It there is a Christmas Rose plant in the garden and we want to have it flowering in the house by Christmas, then special treatment is necessary for, out of doors, it will not flower until January. About two months earlier a bottomless box should be put over the plant and covered with a pane of glass. In the middle of November, before the flowers open, pot it up and bring it indoors where, in a temperature of 60°F (15°C) and in a very dark place the flower stalks can elongate, so that it will open its lovely flowers at the right time.

A flowering plant in the house must be carefully treated in order to keep it in flower as long as possible; a very bright position, not too warm nor too dry an atmosphere and plenty of water are its chief requirements. When the number of flowers decreases, slowly reduce the amount of water until all the leaves have died also. Then put it in a cool room, preferably in a window facing south, where, it can remain until April, then put it out of doors again in a damp place which is not too sunny, but with plenty of humus in the soil. The Christmas Rose should be replanted out of doors without breaking the ball of soil but deep enough to be covered with a layer of humus about 2 in. (5 cm) deep. If the ground is dry ànd poor, it not only wants fertilizer but also loam and leaf-mould. If the plant has been obtained from a florist, it will have been forced and have used up all its strength, so is unlikely to flower the next year but should do so the year following. It will not flower in the house again until the plant is three years old.

Cut flowers of the Christmas Rose last longer if they are put for one night into a bowl of water to which a spoonful of sugar has been added. The following day, slit the stem up about 1 in. (2 cm) and take a small piece off. the bottom before putting it into a vase.

HIBISCUS *Chinese Rose*

This attractive shrub, which comes from China, has in recent years become very popular as an indoor plant that flowers in summer.

The leaves are oblong ovate, pointed at the tip and with a coarsely toothed edge. The flowers appear on long stems in the axils of the leaves, usually from May of June until the autumn. The best known is *Hibiscus rosa sinensis* with very large, loose, carmine flowers with a dark eye. The flowers may be single or double, yellow, pink and white with purple-red eyes. An attractive variety is the variegated *cooperi* with white edges to the leaves and pale pink flowers with a red eye.

Usually the plant is received in bud or flower. It then wants a position with plenty of light, not behind glass, and in full sun. If the air is too dry, the buds will drop. When in bud and in flower, it should not be moved more than necessary or the buds will fall. Whilst growing and flowering the Hibiscus needs plenty of water and fertilizer once a fortnight. In the warmest months it can be put out of doors in a sunny, sheltered place. In long periods of rain or cold, it is better to bring it back into the house again and, in any case, even if the weather is good, it is better to bring it in by September.

The overwintering can be a little difficult, for the plant may droop in a cool room. It is true that it rests in winter but during this period it must be kept in a fairly warm place where the temperature is as even as possible, not below 50°F (12°C) at night.

Give a moderate amount of water during the resting period and it should be at room temperature. Feeding should be stopped entirely until the spring. In any case, do not give it any water when the soil is dark in colour and feels moist.

Usually in the spring the Hibiscus is not in good form and rather bare below. About the end of February, begin to tidy it up. It will need a little pruning and then more water and some feeding. The tips of the branches, about 4 in. (10 cm) long, will root in a pot of leaf-mould and sharp sand, under a plastic cover.

When it grows out of its pot and soon after being pruned, put it in a pot one or two sizes larger, in a mixture of 3 parts leaf-mould, 2 parts fertilizer and 1 part of sharp sand. Or purchase an appropriate potting mixture from the florist. Put a crock at the bottom of the pot with the curved side upwards.

HIPPEASTRUM HYBRIDE *Amaryllis*

A bulb of lasting value is Hippeastrum, with its long, stiff flower stalks which carry the large, showy flowers, red, orange-red, white or striped.

Among amateur growers the name Amaryllis is often used since the scientific name, *Hippeastrum hybride* is not so well known. In most catalogues both names are given to prevent confusion, for some Amaryllis can be grown out of doors whilst Hippeastrum must be grown under glass. There is also a small-flowered type in the trade.

In autumn or winter, purchase one or more bulbs and plant each in a mixture of two parts leaf-mould, one part fertilizer and one part sand; choose a pot an inch or more larger than the bulb and plant it carefully so that one-third of the bulb is covered with soil. Be careful that the long, fleshy roots are not damaged and that the soil is not pressed too tightly round them. Put the pot in a warm room on the mantelpiece at a temperature of 70°F (17-19°C) and give a very little water. If it gets too much water at this time the leaves grow too quickly and the flower buds fail to develop. When the flower bud appears, put it in a sunny window and water more freely as the flower develops, giving fertilizer once a week. The leaves usually appear later and this is a good thing since it means that the plant must still be looked after, for when flowering ceases the real growth of the plant begins; then it wants plenty of water and feeding once a week until the leaves turn yellow about the end of September. Eventually the plant can be put out of doors during the summer months, from the beginning of June to October in a sheltered place where it wants the same treatment as before. At the beginning of October bring it indoors again.

When the leaves have died down, or at least by the first week in October, watering and feeding are discontinued and the pot put in a dry but not too cool place, such as a cupboard in an even temperature. Repot in January. At the same time it will be found that young bulbs with a few roots have developed and these should be removed from the old bulb. They will be flowering size when they are about 7-8 in. (18-20 cm) across. To have the bulbs flowering at Christmas the plants must be dried off in August and repotted in November.

HOYA CARNOSA *Wax Flower*

Hoya carnosa is a climber which is also succulent, and comes from Indonesia. It has a fleshy stem and thick, oval, leathery leaves in the axils of which arise the hemispherical clusters of flowers, pale pink in colour, star-shaped and with a red centre, looking as if made of wax. They also secrete honey which often hangs in drops from the flowers.

Hoya will often flower twice in a year and therefore the stalks of the dead flower heads should be allowed to remain since the new buds are formed on them.

In a room it wants a light, sunny position and can be trained up a pyramid of wire or on a fan-shaped support. It likes plenty of water in the growing period and liquid fertilizer once a fortnight, whilst on warm days the plant can be sprayed. When the buds have formed, the plant should not be turned round or they may drop off.

In winter keep the plant rather drier and do not feed it; although it likes a warm room it will put up with a temperature of 50-60°F (10-15°C). Repotting is seldom necessary but if it should outgrow its pot, then do it in the spring for preference, in leaf-mould with the addition of fertilizer, clay or loam and sharp sand, whilst a layer of crocks at the bottom of the pot will ensure good drainage.

It is easy to propagate by means of cuttings taken in the spring or summer; use one year old shoots about 4-6 in (10-15 cm), put them in sand and leaf-mould and cover with glass. Put the cuttings in a warm place, not in the sun at first, and water sparingly.

Recently a variety, *Hoya carnosa variegata,* has been introduced; it has yellow, marbled leaves and can be used as a climbing or hanging plant and treated like Hoya carnosa itself but the temperature in winter should be above 60°F (15°C).

Hoya is sensitive to mealy bug. The white, fluffy patches should be removed with a brush dipped in methylated spirit. The following day, spray with a mixture of water, soft soap and methylated spirit. Brown specks and a web on the underside of the leaf may mean red spider; spray with an insecticide, repeat after 10-14 days and later if required.

HYDRANGEA MACROPHYLLA

It may well be said that the Hydrangea is one of the most widely distributed of plants. Although not very popular with the present generation, it can hardly be omitted from an old fashioned setting.

In whatever way this plant is regarded, it must still be admitted that few other plants are so satisfactory both in the garden and in the house.

When this plant, which is often known as *Hydrangea hortensis,* is put in the sun, its leaves go limp and droop; this can be remedied by standing it in a pail of water; but this should not be allowed to happen often or the plant may not recover. The cooler the plant can be kept, the longer the flowers will last, always provided it is not in the sun. Whilst in flower it requires plenty of water and a dose of fertilizer at least once a week, in order to lengthen the flowering period.

When the flowers are over, the branches should be cut back so as to leave one or two pairs of leaves only above the old wood, which can be recognised since it is much darker in colour than the younger growth. Then put the Hydrangea in a larger pot, in a mixture of leaf-mould and heavy loam with well-rotted manure or fertilizer added. Do not forget the crocks at the bottom.

Tips that have been cut off, as well as those formed later, can be used during the summer as cuttings. They should be about 4 in. (10 cm) long and will root easily in a flask of water in a warm room. As soon as they have rooted, pot them in the soil mixture given above.

In the summer put the plant out of doors, either in the garden, or on a balcony; in either case in the open air, but not in the mid-day sun. As soon as new growth begins, feed it once a week and give it plenty of water regularly. Now the plant can either begin a new life in the garden or can be brought in again in September and kept in a cool place during the winter.

If too much water is given at this time the plant may develop a disease of the roots so that it will produce weak growths and yellow leaves in the spring.

In January or February it can be brought back into the house where it requires a temperature of 55-65°F (12-18°C) and growth can be encouraged by giving it more and more water and, when growing well, it should be fed.

The blue colour is produced by giving a spoonful of alum on the soil but this is only possible with a pink variety. If obtainable, add alum to the soil.

IMPATIENS SULTANII *Busy Lizzie*

This plant is only seen occasionally in flower shops but it is frequently found in rural areas, often on the window-sills of house after house, where it is known as Busy Lizzie, for it is very floriferous and remains in flower for a long time.

The original form comes from Zanzibar, has carmine flowers and is still seen most often, but there are now new colour varieties available such as salmon, orange, pink, scarlet, white and lilac.

Because it is so easy to propagate by cuttings, it has been widely distributed. Usually the cuttings are rooted in a flask of water in a sunny room so that the development of the roots can be watched.

The nearer the window the plant is placed, the better it will flower, and the more intense will the colour be. If it is not in a bright position, it will flower poorly or not at all, whilst the flowers that do appear soon drop. In winter and spring it wants to be in the sun and during the summer months it should be shaded from the mid-day sun but it should have plenty of fresh air. It can also be put in the garden, either where it gets the morning sun or in a shady place.

Busy Lizzie, because it flowers for so many months, needs plenty of fertilizer, given, preferably, twice a week from May on. During a warm spell, a great deal of water is required, eventually twice a day, whilst in winter, water should be given sparingly since the plant has green juicy stems which tend to rot quickly in damp, cold conditions. Cuttings are taken preferably in the summer, when it is in full growth; they should be 3-4 in. (6-10 cm) long and root easily. When the cutting has rooted in water, pot it up in garden soil, without fertilizer, during the first winter. Once or twice remove the tips of a rooted plant to encourage growth. If, after a year, the plants are found to be too large for the window sill, they may be replaced by cuttings which have come through the winter well and will flower the same summer. If the buds begin to drop, put the plant under a lamp in the evening and in summer plunge the plant in half shade, for choice, otherwise put it in the mid-day sun before an open window.

Greenfly can be treated by spraying with a mixture of soft soap, methylated spirit and water or other suitable insecticides, and repeat after 10-14 days. For the treatment of white fly, see under Fuchsia.

IPOMOEA *Morning Glory*

A departure from the well-known indoor plants is this *Convolvulus* with the long name; it is called *Ipomoea rubrocoerulea praecox,* also known as *I. tricolor* and is rather special among the climbing plants, with its 3-4 in. (8-10 cm) wide, sky-blue flowers, with as many as five or six out at the same time. It is not really an indoor plant but can be used in the house, for this annual climber grows well in a warm, sheltered place. The nurseryman generally keeps it in a light, cool greenhouse and sometimes puts it in a warm sheltered place out of doors.

In contrast to the other plants which are bought fully grown or propagated from cuttings, this can be raised from seed. In March and April, fill a box or pan with ordinary garden soil or, if this is too heavy, add a little sieved leaf-mould and put in on a warm window sill, covered with glass. Keep the soil moist by spraying and wipe the glass daily to remove moisture condensed on it. As soon as the seedlings appear, shade the glass with a piece of paper. Then keep them in the full sun and give neither light nor air. As they grow, give them more air or the seedlings will be drawn. First the seed leaves appear and then the little stems. When they are at that stage, the seedlings can be pricked out into 5 in. pots, putting four or five in each. Scatter sharp sand on the soil and, when potted, they should be put in a very light place in the sun, in front of a window that can be opened when required. It is also possible to sow 4 or 5 seeds in a pot, then they will not need to be pricked out.

As soon as new growth can be seen, the plantlets develop rapidly and will need a support. Some people train them along strings against the window frame, others make a pyramid of wire, fix it in the pot and train the plants round.

The development from bud to open flower is very rapid and can be followed from hour to hour. The prolific flowering compensates for the fact that each flower lasts for one day only. The plant is of no use after it has flowered but it will have given much pleasure throughout the summer. If the leaves get dull in colour with brown spots, the plant has been attacked by red spider and should be sprayed with an insecticide.

IXORA

This is a hot house plant which has been much used as a gift on festive occasions because of its splendid flowers and the way it can be grown in a room where it lasts indefinitely.

It is a shrubby plant, with glossy green leaves bearing at the top of each branch in early summer and autumn many flowers bunched together in spherical clusters, rather like a *Hydrangea. Ixora coccinea* with its scarlet flowers is the only true species still grown, for the rest are hybrids varying in colour from orange-yellow, salmon pink to salmon red.

Only a plant that has been purchased in full bloom does not drop its buds in the house.

It should have a place in the warmest room available, in a light position, but in summer it should be shaded from the mid-day sun. In winter and spring an Ixora can stand the sun. Whilst in flower it must have a regular and plentiful supply of water at room temperature (rain water is best) and fertilizer every fortnight, and if the air in the room is dry, stand the pot on an inverted saucer in a bowl of water. The pot should not touch the water which is intended to moisten the air. Spray the leaves several times a week if necessary.

When the flowers are over, Ixora needs a resting period of about six weeks, so it should be given less water and no feeding and a slightly cooler position but not below 60°F (15°C). After this, cut the plant down to make it a good shape and put it again into a warm place not above 70°F (20°C). At first give it a little water but never cold. As it grows gradually give it fertilizer occasionally and finally every fortnight. In autumn and winter especially it wants a lot of light and, if the house is centrally heated, a moist atmosphere is essential. Besides water in a bowl under the pot, it should be sprayed and saucers of water put on radiators or a kettle of water on the stove are almost as essential as a uniform temperature.

In the spring repot if necessary in leaf-mould, manure or fertilizer and sharp sand, but no lime should be included.

In the warm, dry atmosphere red spider may make its apperance, recognisable by the yellow or brown markings on the leaves and the web on the underside. Spray with an insecticide and repeat after 14 days or when necessary. Do not forget the undersides of the leaves.

KALANCHOE

Kalanchoe blossfeldiana has become very popular as a flowering, succulent plant. Even those who do not care for succulents are charmed by the beautiful clusters of red flowers. Now-a-days other large-leaved and large-flowered types have been developed with orange or red flowers, which are used as cut flowers. Such a large-leaved, orange hybrid is shown at the back of the illustration.

Once in the house it will continue to flower for months but very little water is needed provided the soil remains moist. It should not be watered until the soil becomes light in colour and feels dry, and that depends on the temperature of the room. All too often it is overwatered and this is followed by the rotting of the stem and in consequence the leaves droop. An amateur who sees them drooping naturally thinks the plant wants water and so things get worse and worse until the plant is beyond help.

This Kalanchoe should be watched and, if any sign of rot is noticed, the affected stem should be cut out to prevent the trouble spreading and to save the plant. It also wants a light, airy position such as a window sill since it must not be too warm in winter, but the temperature should not fall below 60°F (15°C) provided it is in a sunny place. Only in the summer should it be shaded from the mid-day sun.

The plant can be increased by cuttings of top shoots in sand, or even by single leaves laid on sand. When they have rooted, pot them up in a mixture of leaf-mould, loam and charcoal and sand. Water and fertilizer should be given carefully; feeding once a month is quite sufficient during the growing and flowering periods.

Kalanchoe is apt to be attacked by mildew which can be recognized by the powdery patches; dust with flower of sulphur but not on a flowering plant. Never use D.D.T.

LANTANA HYBRIDA

A shrubby plant that is found wild on all the islands of the Dutch East Indies and there grows from 2-6 ft. (½-2 meters) high is *Lantana camara.* In our climate Lantana can be grown out of doors in the summer but it is not hardy in the winter and must be protected from frost. The nurserymen now-a-days do not sell the original form but the hybrid *Lantana hybrida* can easily be grown from seed or raised from cuttings. In February the seed can be sown in a box under glass in a warm place in a room. For pot culture the shorter varieties are most in demand.

The box should be filled with sieved leaf-mould, the bottom being covered with coarse leaf-mould, sharp sand and loam and the top layer should consist of a layer 1½ in. (3 cm) deep of sieved leaf-mould. In any case, the soil should be an inch (2 cm) below the edge of the box. Sow the seed and cover lightly. Moisten the soil by spraying and cover with a sheet of glass. Cover the seed with paper until it has germinated and keep it in a warm place. Later, move it into the sun and give more and more light. When they are large enough to handle put the seedlings into pots and turn them so that the seedlings are not drawn. Do not put them out until the end of May in a sheltered, sunny place in a frame or border or in the house in a light place which gets the morning sun, with plenty of fresh air. They want plenty of water when growing and should be transferred to a larger pot and richer soil such as 2 parts leaf-mould, 2 parts fertilizer with 1 part loam and some sharp sand. Whilst they are growing give them fertilizer every fortnight.

Flowering may begin in June and continue till the frost comes, in the meanwhile the Verbena-like blossoms will continue to flower in the house. Being a shrub Lantana need not be thrown away after flowering and the plant can be put out of doors until the frost, that is about the middle of October and then it is brought back into a sunny frame or a room or even a greenhouse. A temperature of 45-50°F (8-10°C) is sufficient, and it should be kept on the dry side. In February put it in a warmer place and new shoots, which can be used as cuttings, will soon root if put in a pot with leaf-mould and sand and covered with plastic. When the cuttings have begun to grow, remove the cover gradually and pinch out the tops. Repeat this several times to make a bushy plant. Further treatment is the same as for plants raised from seed.

MARANTA LEUCONEURA

Some plants are acquired as pot plants but others are more often met with as part of a floral arrangement and thus *Maranta leuconeura* variety *kerchoveana* is usually received as an addition to a decorative bowl or basket. It has emerald green leaves with dark, velvety spots between the veins. Since the spots look like finger prints, its common name is 'Ten Commandments'. When young the leaves are tightly rolled and look like cigarettes sticking out of the centre of the plant. It comes from the tropical regions of Africa and America and therefore needs a moist atmosphere. It is best to stand it on an inverted saucer in a bowl of water which keeps the air round it moist all the time. The water level must be lower than the base of the pot. It should be syringed regularly, using a fine spray, and this is better than pouring too much water on the soil, especially in winter as, otherwise, the plant may rot round the collar. In spring and summer it can be given fertilizer every fortnight. During the winter keep it warm but rather less moist and in the spring, repot if necessary and the plant can then be divided.

Maranta likes a porous soil and a shallow pan or bowl. First put a layer of crocks at the bottom and over this a mixture of peat, leaf-mould, turfy loam and sand. Do not pack the soil round the plant too firmly or it will cease to be porous. Put the plant in a warm place and start it into growth, such as on a mantlepiece, and cover it with glass.

Dry heat or sunshine may cause red spider which can be recognised by the white flecks or yellow and brown coloration, and sometimes a web. Spray with an insecticide and repeat every fortnight. Do not forget the underside of the leaf.

The illustration shows *Maranta leuconeura kerchoveana* on the right. In the centre is *Calathea makoyana (Maranta makoyana)*. On the left is *Calathea insignis*. The last two are closely related and need more warmth, 50°F (10°C), and a moister atmosphere.

MONSTERA DELICIOSA

Monstera deliciosa is an unusual and striking plant, sometimes erroneously called *Philodendron pertusum,* which on account of its ability to adapt itself, may be considered an ideal house plant.

It comes from Guatemala and only when mature does it produce flowers which somewhat resemble Arum Lilies. The true form of the leaves is very remarkable, for the leaf edge is so deeply cut and the leaf itself so irregularly perforated, that it appears to be full of holes.

It has already been said that Monstera is very adaptable and not at all particular about its surroundings. The best temperature in winter is 55-70°F (12-20°C). In summer it naturally needs more warmth than in the winter months and the water given should be at room temperature. It should not be watered when the soil is still dark in colour and feels moist. Otherwise a normal room temperature is suitable and it can stand the dry air of a room if it is sprayed in dry weather and the leaves sponged once a week. In summer it should be kept out of the sun.

When the plant is growing well, aerial roots gradually develop along the stems; they should not be removed, in fact they rather enhance the attractiveness of the plant. If a climbing plant is wanted, put it against a wall to which the aerial roots will soon attach themselves firmly. During the growing period give it fertilizer once a fortnight.

If Monstera gets too tall it can easily be reduced by cutting it in two. The lower half will then make new shoots and, if cut below aerial roots, the upper half will grow on in a mixture of coarse leaf-mould, fertilizer and sand. The top can also be rooted in water in a warm, shady place. The aerial roots can hang down into the water. Yellow or brown flecks or a web suggest red spider and should be sprayed with an insecticide repeated in a fortnight if necessary. Spray the undersides of the leaves also.

NEOREGELIA *Bromeliad*

This handsome rosette Bromeliad with creamy white bracts, longitudinally striped with yellow and red which surround the insignificant inflorescence, is known under various names. The present-day name is *Neoregelia carolinae* 'Tricolor', but it is also known as *Aregelia* and *Nidularium*. It comes from the virgin forests of Brazil and prefers a warm, shady hothouse to the dry air of a room. It wants a position with plenty of light to retain its beautiful colour and therefore from March to September should be shaded from the mid-day sun for an hour or two but it likes the morning sun.

As well as water at room temperature on the soil, it likes tepid water in the leaf rosette. If the room is warmed by a stove, it will be much cooler by the wall, then, in winter the rosette need not be watered daily. If there is central heating, it can be watered all through the year. In spring and summer it can be given fertilizer once a fortnight; in winter less water is needed and no fertilizer.

A moist atmosphere is desirable and can be provided by damping down with water from a radiator or a kettle. The best winter temperature is between 60-70°F (15-20°C) but in summer it should not rise above 75°F (25°C),

Cuttings taken of branches produce poor roots and these should be put in a pot with a light soil mixture. If a piece of the main stem or bark is put in a garden frame in damp sphagnum and tied firmly, it will grow quickly.

If they are to be grown in a pot, then take a small one, put a layer of crocks at the bottom and fill in with a light soil mixture such as leaf-mould, sphagnum, loam and sharp sand. If necessary, use a small pot so that it will not grow too large. The best time to repot is late in the spring, that is towards the end of April, if it is not showing flower.

For some amateurs it is a disappointment that the small lilac flowers do not grow above the rosette but that is no mistake in the treatment of the plant, it is normal and the attraction is the bright red colour assumed by the inner leaves during and after flowering.

It can be increased by young shoots taken from the base, but also from seed. A Bromeliad flowers only once and then dies but may live on for a few months and sometimes longer. Young shoots develop at the base and should be taken off when they are half the size of the mother plant.

NEPHROLEPIS *Fern*

Not many plants will last for long in a dark room and, until we can build our houses to our own designs, we are obliged to put up with some rooms that are unfortunately situated but which we should like to brighten up with flowers or plants. Happily ferns are a solution for, as woodland plants in nature, they are already adapted to live in the shade.

Nephrolepis especially, which wants but little light, is a splendid subject for the dullest room. With its finely divided, feathery fronds, which are attractively crimped, it is one of the most decorative of foliage plants. In the illustration are shown from left to right: *Nephrolepis exaltata* 'Roosevelti', *Nephrolepis cordifolia* and *Nephrolepis exaltata.*

Although a Nephrolepis needs but little light, yet it must not be pushed into the darkest corner for obviously it cannot live with no light at all. Like all ferns, it prefers a moist atmosphere which can be provided by regular spraying. A temperature of 55-65°F (16-18°C) is recommended.

Sometimes excellent results are obtained by standing the plant on an inverted saucer in a bowl of water or on a rubber dish with ridges, so that the water does not reach the pot. This provides for humidity round the leaves. A general rule for watering cannot be given since in any room the moisture content is different. Use rain water for preference. The ball of soil must not dry out.

If this should happen, then the pot should be stood in a pail of tepid water, even above the top of the pot, until it ceases to bubble. Then take it out and return it to its former position.

In spring and summer give fertilizer once a fortnight.

Among the lower leaves of the varieties *Nephrolepis cordifolia* and *N. exaltata,* runners will develop, on which young plants will form which, when large enough, should be taken off and potted up in a mixture that suits all ferns, that is woodland soil with well-rotted manure or fertilizer and sharp sand; this should not be pressed down too firmly. Above all, do not forget to put crocks at the bottom.

Fully grown plants should only be repotted when they are growing out of their pots and, for preference, early in the New Year. First remove the old soil from the roots and then put the plant into a pot that is not too large in a mixture given above.

NERIUM OLEANDER

This plant, which grows wild in the Mediterranean Region, is commonly seen in our country also. Most holiday makers bring back from the sunny south cuttings taken in their natural surroundings of this flowering shrub. These cuttings can easily be rooted in a vase of water in a sunny room. When taken in June, by August or September, they will have become flowering plants. Often they get no further than buds which, for lack of warmth, fail to open and soon dry up.

If the cutting has been successfully rooted, pot it up in a good soil. That sold by florists, if obtainable, suits them very well but the less ideal their position is, the more they will benefit from a rich soil. A mixture of heavy loam with fertilizer and sharp sand gives good results but do not put them into too small a pot, but with a good layer of crocks at the bottom.

Give the plant a sunny position and, about September or October, put it in a warm, sheltered place. When it is growing, occasionally take the tips off the plant so as to make it branch and so produce more flowers, but the single or double flowers at the top of the shoots should be left. The colour varies from purple-red, cherry-red, pink or salmon-pink, flesh-coloured or white. The flowers generally last from July to October. As the buds form, remove the side shoots below them so that the sap can flow up to the buds. After flowering the plant can be cut hard back. In spring or summer it will want a good deal of water, which should not be too cold, for it takes water up with difficulty if it is colder than the soil. Rainwater is much the best. Spray the leaves and buds and give fertilizer once a fortnight.

During the winter the plant should not be kept too warm but the temperature should not fall below 40°F (5°C). During this period give a little luke warm water and plenty of light is required.

It has been mentioned that the Oleander wants a large pot and, if it has outgrown it, then in the spring put it into a tub. Once this has been done, repotting will seldom be necessary but do not forget to feed the plant.

Above all, look out for mealy bug and scale which can be treated with methylated spirit. Every 10-14 days give it fertilizer if necessary.

NERTERA DEPRESSA *Coral Moss*

Coral Moss is only a modest little plant whose leaves are not particularly attractive nor has it a wealth of flowers, but nevertheless it can be very decorative when covered with its orange berries that appear in August. The orange fruits that follow the inconspicuous greenish-white blossoms are, in relation to the size of the plant, comparatively large, similar in shape and size to a small pea. The gaily decorated plant can be enjoyed until late autumn and afterwards it should be overwintered in a cool place, free from frost.

If it gets too much sun, the leaves will grow too fast and the berries will not show to good advantage; therefore a light but slightly shaded position should be chosen and the watering must be done carefully as the leaves are easily damaged underneath. To prevent this, it is better to put it in a saucer of water and to use the syringe as little as possible and never when the plant is in flower, otherwise no fruits will set. About May and June, when it is in bloom, the little green flowers should have a brush passed over them daily to ensure the setting of the fruits. A medium temperature of 50°F (12-13°C) should give the best results.

Nertera is best grown in a low bowl with plenty of drainage, and the soil a light mixture of leaf-mould and sand. When the plant gets too large, it can be divided, about September or October, in any case after the fruits have fallen, or in spring, after the resting period.

Not everyone is successful in getting berries on this plant, especially if it is in a position that is too warm and sunny, and yet a Coral Moss which does not flower can be used as a hanging plant, which many growers like, but it is more satisfactory if it does produce berries. The plant is very like *Helxine soleirolii,* a small, mat-forming plant which, however, never produces berries.

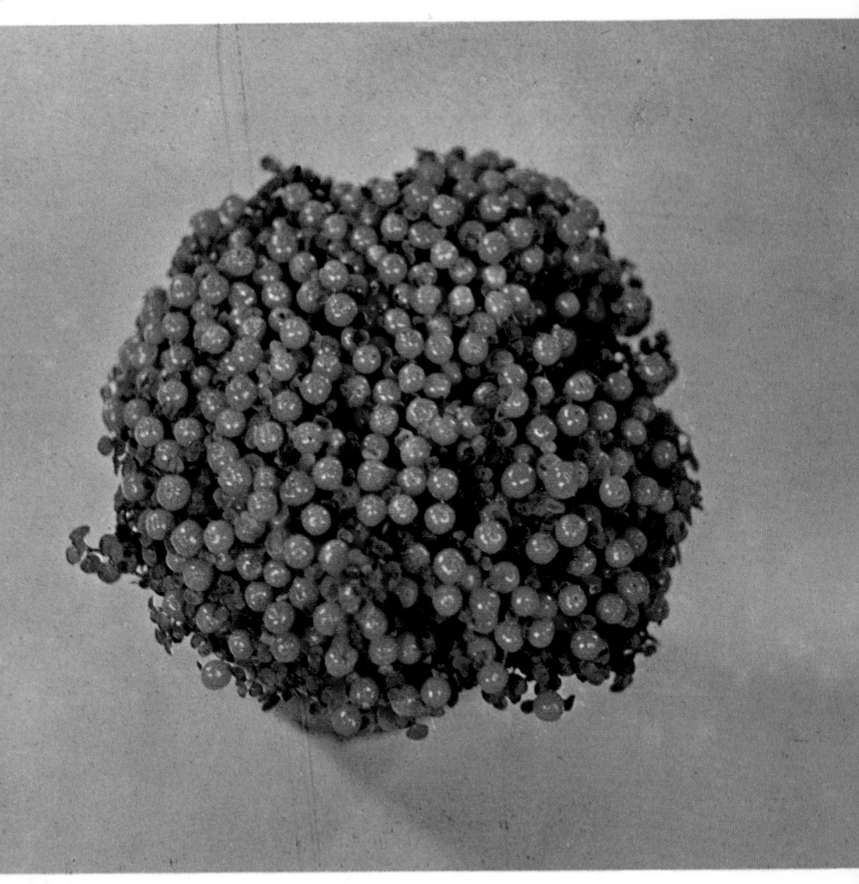

ODONTOGLOSSUM GRANDE *Orchid*

It is gradually being realised that it is quite possible to grow Orchids in the house but they are not recommended often enough so that it is only occasionally that they are seen in a dwelling house. One of the most beautiful orchids for a living room is *Odontoglossum grande,* with curiously marked flowers in a colour combination of brown and yellow; there may be four to six blooms on one stem and these will open from September to November. Odontoglossum is one of the epiphytic orchids which, in contrast to terrestrial orchids, lives on trees and, in consequence, has a quite different type of root and leaf. At the base of the leaves the stem is thickened and, in Odontoglossum, it is very broad, oval in shape and greyish green in colour, with the underside flecked with violet. This is a reservoir for water and food which, in these orchids, carries them through the dry period. These 'pseudo-bulbs' as they are called, each bear two leaves.

In a room this orchid wants plenty of light, but not too much sun nor too warm a place. In summer 60-65°F (15-17°C) is best, in winter 45-50°F (7-12°C). From March to September, shade it from the sun. In the summer when growth is active, give it plenty of water and once a fortnight fertilizer, gradually reducing the amount but taking care that the newly formed pseudo-bulbs do not dry up. Rainwater should be used, for preference.

As the buds form, more and more water should be given and plenty of water at room temperature when the flowers appear.

After flowering, from December to May, no water is required. A moist atmosphere is, however, necessary and therefore the pot is, throughout the year, stood on an inverted saucer in a bowl of water but the water should not reach the pot. Orchids do well if they are sprayed overhead daily, except when they are in flower.

They should be repotted every two years in April and May when the young shoot is at least 2 in. (4 cm) high, in a mixture of equal parts of chopped sphagnum and fern roots. The pot should not be too large but filled with crocks for one-third of its depth. The upper surface should have a layer of living sphagnum over it.

PAPHIOPEDILUM

Cypripedium, Lady's Slipper

A terrestrial orchid, which is suitable for growing in the house, is the Lady's Slipper. It is best to start with a plant that is in flower which, for *Paphiopedilum insigne,* is during the winter months. The flowers last a long time, from November to February. It gets its name from the unusual shape of the lip which protrudes from the flower and looks like a little, greenish slipper with a bronze sheen. In winter the plant is best kept on a window sill in a fairly warm room, about 55-60°F (12-15°C), in a moist atmosphere which is provided by standing the pot on an inverted saucer in a bowl of water. In summer it wants a temperature of 65°F (18°C) for choice, in a window facing north-east or north-west. And if that is not possible, then behind a curtain or sunblind during the mid-day sun.

Whilst in flower it should be kept really moist and sprayed frequently, but not over the plant. After flowering it still wants spraying but not too much ventilation. Directly after flowering the plant should be repotted every other year, which is not an easy job and is, perhaps, best left to the florist. If one wants to do it oneself, then a mixture of chopped sphagnum, chopped fern root and half-rotted oak leaves will be found suitable. The pot should be filled one-third full of crocks, after having been scrubbed clean. The roots of the plant should have all the old soil removed as carefully as possible, then put it into the soil mixture so that it stands above the rim of the pot. Finally the soil is covered with a layer of living sphagnum. Always use a small pot. After repotting, spray the leaves well but do not water the soil. In May keep it very moist and give more fresh air. In September reduce the amount of water and, as soon as buds have formed, keep it in a temperature at or above 55-60°F (12-15°C). The pot should be stood on an inverted saucer in a bowl of water, so that the water does not reach the pot.

Lady's Slippers with green leaves are more suitable as house plants than those which have marbled leaves. The latter need, in winter, a temperature about 65°F (18°C) and, when growing, 70-75°F (20-22°C).

PASSIFLORA *Passion Flower*

A climbing plant from Tropical America which attaches itself by means of branchlets that have been converted into tendrils and arise in the axils of the 5-7 lobed leaves. But the flowers are the greatest attraction, which no one would ever forget once they have seen them in their full glory.

This remarkable flower derives its name, according to legend, because it symbolizes the crucifixion. The flowers have in the centre a crown of threads which resemble Christ's crown of thorns. The pistil and stamens are thought to represent the hammer and nails and the style the cross.

The best-known species is the blue Passion Flower, *Passiflora caerulea* which, together with the white variety, 'Constance Elliot', are the most suitable for growing indoors, whilst the blue Passion Flower does well in summer against a sunny wall where it will grow very large and may produce as many as 80 flowers.

In the house it wants a very light position in a conservatory or room. It grows best in a sunny place where it gets plenty of fresh air in summer. It flowers chiefly in the summer months and, whilst growing and flowering, needs a lot of water and fertilizer once a fortnight.

Since it climbs quickly, it needs support in the form of a pyramid made of wire or of sticks round the edge of the pot, to which it can be tied.

In winter it does not need to be too warm and a temperature of 45-50°F (6-10°C) is sufficient. At this time it is resting and can be kept drier, with no fertilizer. Plants which have been out of doors can be brought into an unheated room at the beginning of October. If the winter is not too cold, the plant can be given a covering of loam or leaf-mould, or branches piled on it. When the ground thaws out in the spring, the plant can be cut back, which encourages new shoots; the tips cut off 4-6 in. (10-15 cm) long can be used as cuttings and rooted in water or in leaf-mould mixed with sharp sand, and kept in a warm place.

It wants repotting when it has outgrown the pot it is in and this can be done at the same time as the pruning. Use good soil made up of leaf-mould, turfy loam and fertilizer. A good layer of crocks at the bottom of the pot is most important.

PELARGONIUM ZONALE *Geranium*

Although few amateurs know the name Pelargonium in connection with the popular Geranium, yet this is the correct name; the confusion in the names has arisen because the plant belongs to the family *Geraniaceae.* Pelargoniums are being used more and more in the house, though previously used chiefly as bedding plants.

The dwarf variety *Pelargonium hortorum* 'Black Vesuvius' is an exception, for it does not do well in the garden but may be considered an ideal house plant, especially as it remains in flower for about nine months of the year. It is not particular about the conditions but the lighter and sunnier the place where it is put, the better coloured will be its leaves, which in this variety are brownish in colour, in contrast with the brilliant scarlet flowers.

In summer a Pelargonium wants plenty of water but not on the leaves or flowers as they tend to rot easily; to encourage flowering give it fertilizer once a week. But in any case do not water when the soil is dark in colour. Little water is needed in winter but it should not be stopped entirely for, in a light, warm place, even in winter, the flowers may begin to develop.

In the spring it is advisable to repot, for the long-continued flowering takes a lot of nourishment out of the soil. Small pots should be used as a rule, and filled with sandy leaf-mould. At the end of February or beginning of March, cut the plant back.

Cuttings may be taken either in spring or in August; choose well developed shoots 3-4 in (6-10 cm) long and remove the lowest leaves. The cut should be made just below a leaf. Lay the cuttings aside for a few days to dry the cut surface and then put them into sandy soil.

The ordinary *Pelargonium zonale* does well in summer if the pot is sunk out of doors in the morning sun. Water it if the weather is dry and give it fertilizer now and then. In a long period of drought give it plenty of water and fertilizer. Bring it in by the middle of October and put it in a light, sunny, cool room. At first water it once a week but do not feed it. During a frost give no water; at the end of February or in March, put it in a warmer place in a sunny room. At the same time repot it in the mixture given above. Do not put it out till the middle of May, otherwise keep it in a well ventilated room. For treatment of White Fly, see under *Fuchsia.*

PELLAEA *Fern*

It is as well to mention that Pellaea is a fern, for *Pellaea rotundifolia,* illustrated here, has the fronds cut into round, leathery segments and does not look much like a fern, but it is well known as an underplanting for bowls.

The plant remains low and is suitable for a small window sill where it can hang down. It grows more in breadth than in height. It comes from New Zealand and this type of fern is not so exacting with regard to moisture and warmth as are the tropical ferns. Like all ferns it does not like full sun but in winter and spring and autumn it can endure sun morning and evening provided it is screened from the sun at mid-day.

Pellaea wants plenty of water in the soil, may be sprayed in warm weather or occasionally put out in the rain. When growing it should be treated as a fern and given fertilizer every fortnight.

In the winter it can be kept in a moderately warm room and, since it is one of the hardy ferns, it will stand the dry air of a room. The cooler it is the less water it will require but all ferns like a moderately damp soil.

If the edges of the fronds dry up, the room is either too dry or too warm or the plant is getting too much sun. In that case it should be stood on an inverted saucer in a bowl of water so that the water cannot reach the pot. This will give a damp atmosphere round the pot. Use the syringe regularly.

The roots of these plants spread sideways rather than downwards so that they are especially good for planting in bowls; if not in a bowl, they prefer a deep pan rather than a pot.

Repotting is only necessary when they outgrow their pots or are in the way of other plants in bowls. Plenty of crocks should be used to prevent the soil becoming sour and the roots rotting. Pellaea wants an open but nourishing soil, such as 3 parts of leaf-mould, 2 parts fertilizer and 1 part peat.

Repotting is best done in the early spring when the old soil should be removed and the long roots disentangled. The compost should not be too firm. After repotting, put the plant in a warmer place, water moderately and keep it out of the sun.

PEPEROMIA

The Pepper family gives us, not only useful plants such as pepper, but also various attractive, ornamental plants which are noted for the beautiful markings on their leaves. Although the flowers are of secondary importance, yet the typical, long, thin brown, green or white flower spikes are amusing. The variety is considerable and many different kinds are used in plant bowls. In the illustration several that are useful indoor plants are shown. In the foreground is *Peperomia glabella foliis variegatis* with spreading growth; in the background from left to right: *Peperomia tithymaloides foliis variegatis, P. caperata* and *P. sandersii.*

Peperomias are tropical plants which used to be grown in a hot house, therefore a moist atmosphere should be provided indoors. Peperomia is a real shade lover and the leaves lose their freshness in the sun. But they do not not like too dark a place either, especially in winter when they must be kept in a warm room. A steaming kettle on the fire or bowls of water on the radiator will help, or the plant can be put on an inverted saucer in a bowl of water; the base of the pot should not touch the water which evaporates round the plant. In a plant bowl this may not be possible, then spray the leaves of the plant overhead. The soil should be kept moist and the room temperature in winter can be a little warmer. When it is growing give fertilizer every fortnight. Some people have success in winter with daily spraying and then giving no more water on the soil. But this is a question of personal experience and every room has a different atmosphere to which the plant must adapt itself.

In cooler surroundings, a chilly atmosphere and water that is too cold, the Peperomia may lose its leaves. A temperature of 60-65°F (16-18°C) is best. If necessary, Peperomia should be repotted in the spring in a porous soil mixture, in not too large a pot. Leaf-mould, peat and sharp sand gives good results and, above all, do not forget to put a layer of crocks on the bottom of the pot. In the spring cuttings can be taken from a fully grown leaf with a piece of stalk about 1 in. (2 cm) long; put it in sandy leaf-mould and covered with glass. Then put it under a plastic cover for three weeks. Give it a warm place, by the stove or radiator, to encourage growth and keep it fairly moist, using tepid water.

PHILODENDRON SCANDENS

This is a modern climbing plant often used now-a-days and one of the most satisfactory of indoor plants. It belongs to the same family as *Monstera* and *Scindapsus aureus* with which it has much in common.

The leaves are heart-shaped, dark green, leathery, shining and wavy between the veins; they are heart-shaped and stand at right angles to the long leaf stalks. The stem lies flat against the wall and often attaches itself to it. Otherwise a few drawing pins may be used to train it up, but be careful not to pierce the stalks.

It does not want much light and prefers, in summer, to be in a cool, sunless room, eventually framing the door or hanging from the mantelpiece. Not much water is needed, only when the soil is light in colour and feels dry to the touch. Once a month give it fertilizer. A Philodendron can stand great fluctuations of temperature and, when used on the mantelpiece, can remain there even if the stove is alight; no harm will come to it and the leaves will not fall off. In winter the temperature should not fall below 50°F (12°C). Care must be taken that it does not get too wet; use only water at room temperature when the soil is light in colour and therefore dry.

The leaves should be sponged occasionally, or gently wiped with a duster. It does not need a resting period but grows faster in the summer.

Repotting is seldom necessary; it is enough if the top layer of soil is removed in spring and replaced by leaf-mould and sharp sand, and well-rotted manure or fertilizer.

The plant can be propagated by cuttings. Should it grow too tall 4-6 in. (10-15 cm) can be cut off the top and put 1 in. (2 cm) deep in a small pot filled with leaf-mould and sharp sand. The rest of the stem can be cut into lengths and rooted. Put the cuttings in a warm place, out of the sun and cover them with glass or a plastic bag where they should be left for three weeks.

If the leaves develop brown or yellow spots and there is a web on the underside, the plant probably has red spider. This should be sprayed with one of the insecticides available; repeat in 10-14 days and as often as necessary. Also spray the underside of the leaf.

PILEA CADIEREI

A new arrival amongst the foliage plants which now-a-days is much used in plant bowls and, as a house plant, is a great acquisition.

It is distinguished by the ovate leaves which end in points, olive coloured with silvery markings, more or less striped along the veins. The glossy, leathery leaves are in pairs alternating up the stem, and the growth is shrubby. Older plants sometimes become pendent so that the stems hang down over the window sill. Occasionally small bunches of brownish flowers appear on the top of the stems.

Coming from Indo-China, it is used to a good deal of heat, 60-65°F (16-18°C) and should be put in a sunny window where, in the spring and summer only, it should be shaded from the mid-day sun. However, it does quite well facing north or north-east but in a cold winter the lowest leaves turn black and fall off.

It is very suitable where there is central heating but it will want a lot of water in winter and, above all, a moist atmosphere, so the plant should be sprayed. In any case the water should be at room temperature and should be given whenever the soil is light in colour and, therefore, dry. Whilst it is growing give it fertilizer every fortnight to keep the large leaves in good condition. Since, during the winter, it will have lengthened and lost most of its leaves, in March or April it should be cut back. It regains its shrubby form again; the pruning does not follow definite rules, so take off what is necessary. Usually the leafy tops are used to make good cuttings. They should be 3-4 in. (6-10 cm) long and will soon root in a flask of water in a sunny room, or in a small pot filled with leaf-mould and sharp sand, preferably under glass or plastic cover. Later repot into rich soil such as equal parts of leaf-mould, and fertilizer to which has been added turfy loam. Take out the tips as it grows to make a well-shaped plant

The same soil mixture can be used to repot the old plant after it has been cut back and, as it will not be in good shape, it can be planted out of doors during the summer months, but not before the end of May or beginning of June, otherwise the edges of the leaves may be damaged by the cold.

During September bring it into a warm room in full light and not shaded from the sun with plenty of ventilation. Gradually get it used to the higher temperature. Plants kept indoors in the summer need plenty of fresh air.

PLATYCERIUM BIFURCATUM

Platycerium alcicorne, Stag-horn Fern

There are about ten varieties of the Stag-horn Fern known and most of them have handsome, indented leaves which look like antlers; at the base of the plant another type of leaf occurs, round and shield-shaped, that curves over the roots and prevents them from drying out and gives support to the antler-like fronds. In a young plant, this covering is felt-like and greyish-green in contrast to the shining, dark green of the other leaves. After a time these sheathing leaves take on a brown colour which does not by any means spoil the effect.

The female fronds are fertile and bear the spores by which the plant is increased, the shield fronds are sterile and can therefore produce no spores. There is a new cultivar 'Wilhelmina Regina' in which the fertile fronds stand up like a fan.

The plant comes from Australia where it lives on the branches and stems of trees, hence it is often grown as a hanging plant on cork or wood.

If one wants to try it on cork, lay on the hollow side of a slab of cork a mixture of finely chopped moss, peat and loam and fasten the plant on with copper wire so that the roots are in the mixture and the wire is made fast between the sheath and the antler leaves. The atmosphere should not be too dry and the winter temperature not below 60°F (15°C) and can be higher. Plunge it occasionally in a pail of tepid water. The hairy leaves should not be sponged. Spray in the air over the plant.

Sometimes it is attacked by scale insects whose round, brown scales should be dabbed with methylated spirit by means of a brush. The following day, spray with a mixture of soft soap, methylated spirit and water. Repeat when necessary. D.D.T. can also be used.

PRIMULA MALACOIDES

A species which is not so well known as *Primula obconica* is the small-flowered *Primula malacoides* which, by the lavish display of its blossom, makes ample compensation for the small size of its flowers. These are similar in shape to those of *P. obconica,* are arranged in tiers up the flower stem and are produced throughout the winter months from January to April, the colours being lilac, carmine, pink or white, according to the varieties. The whole inflorescence is covered with a white powder.

It is not difficult to grow in a room if it is remembered that the plant does not like full sun and prefers a cool place in a north or north-east window where there is plenty of air.

It is seldom a success because it is often grown too warm so that the flowers and leaves dry up. It is often a disappointment to people that it does not like the warm, dry air of a living room. It remains in flower longest at a temperature of 50°F (10°C) and not above 55°F (12°C). Give it fresh air daily.

Primula malacoides is not so easy to keep for another year as *Primula sinensis* and *Primula obconica* but it can be done and the true plant lover will like to try.

Considering that the plant flowers so profusely, it goes without saying that it will need plenty of nourishment so give it plenty of water when it is brought into the house and fertilizer weekly till after flowering. Remove flowers as they die off to lengthen the flowering period. The plant should then be given a rest, so put it in a cooler place and give it very little water. During the summer months put it out of doors in a shady place where it can be watered. September is the time to bring it into the house again and then, if necessary, it should be repotted in garden soil mixed with peat and light loam. Leaf-mould should not be used for Primulas, especially oak leaf-mould which is definitely harmful to these plants. In October feeding can begin again and the plant put back in its former position in a cool room, if possible, not above 50-55°F (10-12°C).

PRIMULA OBCONICA

It is true to say that *Primula obconica* is one of the most satisfactory flowering plants in the house for, with very little care, it will flower the whole year round. For choice it should not be put in the sun but in a bright position such as a window facing north or north-east where it should be kept moist. A winter temperature of 50-60°F (10-15°C) is best. As the flowers die, remove the heads at once or the plant may stop flowering. On account of its prolific and prolonged flowering, it obviously needs a lot of feeding and therefore liquid fertilizer should be given regularly once a week. Unless it is fed, the later flowers will become paler and paler and the leaves smaller and smaller. During the summer months the plant should be rested, so put it in a cool a place as possible, give it less water and fertilizer every three weeks. In August feeding is stopped entirely until October when it can be given weekly again.

It is advisable first to repot the Primula, not in leaf-mould but in heavy garden soil mixed with peat and sharp sand with the addition of well-rotted manure or fertilizer. If the old pot is well scrubbed it can be used again. Leaf-mould in the soil mixture may cause the edges of the leaves to turn yellow if they are exposed to the mid-day sun in spring and summer. Do not put the plant too deep when repotting or the soft centre may rot.

The only objection to this otherwise most attractive plant is that the glandular hairs on the stem causes a rash on the hand with some people. Anyone who is susceptible to this should wear gloves when handling the plant; if the skin comes in contact, a remedy such as a soothing ointment should be applied quickly. Fortunately many of the newer varieties have almost lost this objectionable character so that anyone can grow the plant indoors safely. White fly, which now and then occurs on Primulas, can be treated with D.D.T. or other suitable insecticides.

PRIMULA SINENSIS

One of the best Primulas for a room is still *Primula sinensis,* which is seen less often than formerly and yet, if only for its brilliant colour, is more valuable than any other Primula. Thanks to the work of nurserymen in recent years, the loveliest shades and colours have been produced such as pure white, flesh pink, blood red, orange, blue purple, and many intermediate shades. The plants flower from October to April and, if a flowering Primula is bought, it should be given a place in full light but not in the sun, for example, in a window that faces north or north-east, where it should be given plenty of water and fresh air. In a dry warmth or in the sun, the leaves turn yellow and the flowering period is shortened. Dead flowers should be removed at once. Since it flowers for such a long time it wants a lot of nourishment, so fertilizer should be given every fortnight. Plants that have finished flowering are best repotted in the spring; they are then put not too deep and, if the plant has several crowns, it can be divided by cutting through with a sharp knife, and the parts potted up separately, using small pots. This species has a tendency to fall over, then it must not be planted more deeply, when heart-rot may develop, but stakes of iron wire can be used to prop it up.

Anyone who has a cold frame will find it interesting to grow these Primulas from seed. Since they dislike sun at any time, they should be sown in a shady place, in a mixture of weathered turf with peat and sharp sand, avoiding leaf-mould since no Primula will grow in it. Cover with glass and keep the seeds moist by spraying. Prick the seedlings out once, then put them into small pots and leave them in a cold frame from which frost is excluded during the winter and in spring bring them into a cool room where the temperature of 50-55°F (10-13°C) can be maintained.

PTERIS

Besides the sturdiest of the Ferns, the well-known Holly Fern, there are others which do very well in a room in the genus Pteris. The best known species are *Pteris multifida (serrulata)*, *Pteris tremula* and *Pteris cretica*. In the illustration, on the left is *Pteris tremula* next to varieties of *Pteris cretica*. Of all the varieties, *Pteris tremula* is the least sturdy and, in appearance, resembles our woodland Ferns; it has the same requirements, that is, a rather shady positon and a moist atmosphere, which can be provided by standing the pot on an inverted saucer in a bowl of water. In spring and summer, it can be put out in the rain.

The other species of Pteris are much sturdier, as can be seen from their appearance; their leaves are firm and rather leathery. They are able to withstand the dry atmosphere and warmth of the living room, but they can also stand a moderately warm room, about 45-55°F (8-12°C). In the summer the plants should be kept well watered and it is important to spray them regularly. They want liquid fertilizer once a fortnight. In the winter little water is required; it depends on their position. The soil should not dry out entirely since woodland soil, of which it is largely composed, once it gets dry is difficult to moisten again. If the soil dries out the pot should be stood in a pail of tepid water over the rim until it ceases to bubble.

When the plant needs repotting use, for choice, woodland soil or leaf-mould mixed with sharp sand and fertilizer. This should be done in the spring. First shake the old soil out of the roots, put in a good layer of crocks for drainage and do not press the soil down too hard. Then put it in a warmer place but out of the sun.

A pest to which Pteris is susceptible is scale. To deal with it the round, brown scales should be moistened with methylated spirit. The following day take them off, or spray with a solution of nicotine in water. Repeat when necessary. Do not use D.D.T.

RHOEO DISCOLOR

A new house plant which comes from Mexico and is related to the familiar *Tradescantia*. With its rosette of metallic, shining, green leaves, which are purple on the undersides, it reminds one of a Bromeliad. There is also a variety with yellow, striped leaves known as *Rhoeo discolor 'Fittata'*.

In America this bi-coloured plant is known as 'Moses in the Cradle', a name for which it has to thank the typical tuber-like white flowers at the base of the leaves, half hidden by the boat-shaped bracts. It is also compared with a little bird that is busy coming out of the egg. In either case, a fascinating appearance among the house plants.

It is rather more difficult than most of the *Tradescantias* but is successful in a well heated room with plenty of light. In winter a temperature of 65°F (18°C) is suitable, which should not fall below 60°F (15°C) in the night. Rhoeo also wants a moist atmosphere. This means that it should not only have the soil watered but also be sprayed over the leaves with water that must be at room temperature; according to the more or less dry warmth of the room, this should be given daily or every other day.

A kettle of water on the stove and bowls of water on the radiators will eventually evaporate and will increase the moisture in the air. Take care that winter is really over before pouring too much or too cold water on the soil.

In spring and summer the plant wants a moderate amount of water, whilst the spraying should be continued. Then give it fertilizer every fortnight until October. From March to September shade it from the mid-day sun.

When it outgrows its pot, in spring or summer, put it in another pot one or two sizes larger, in a mixture of leaf-mould, fertilizer, loam and sharp sand. Cover the hole at the bottom with a crock, curved side upwards.

Rhoeo can be propagated from seed or by cuttings. In practice the amateur can only take cuttings. These can be taken in February and March and put in a pot with leaf-mould and sharp sand. Give it water and cover with a plastic bag. Growth will be assisted if the pot is on a warm base such as a stove or radiator. After three or four weeks, water it if necessary. Remove the cover as soon as growth begins. It is probable that the cuttings will all be rooted in 3-4 weeks. Then slowly remove the plastic bag, to get the cuttings used to the dry air of the room. When they are growing well, repot in the mixture given above.

RICHARDIA *Zantedeschia, Calla, Arum*

Although every one knows the Arum Lily as a cut flower, there are still only a few homes where it is used as an indoor plant. Yet it is not difficult to manage and can be grown by anyone. One of the sturdiest varieties for a room is 'Perle von Stuttgart', long lived and free flowering. If one wants to experiment, then begin with the dry corms, which are put into not too small pots at the beginning of July, filled with a mixture of 2 parts heavy loam, 1 part leaf-mould, 1 part garden soil and some fertilizer.

Since the corms root from the top also, they must not be planted too high. If a cold frame in the garden is available, the simplest way is to sink the pots in the frame, water well if dry and, when growth begins, give fertilizer. Cover the pots with a layer of peat dust to prevent drying out in warm weather. Keep in the shade, not in full sun. By the end of September or beginning of October, according to the weather, put them in a sunny frame or into a light room.

Provided the pots are not kept too warm (a temperature of 55-60°F (12-15°C) is enough) and they are in a light place, failure is almost impossible. When the plant is growing well it needs plenty of water and, from September to February, fertilizer once a week, and thereafter until the plant has finished flowering, twice a week. The chief flowering period is between February and April. The leaves should be sponged weekly with tepid water.

After flowering, the resting period begins, from the middle of May to the beginning of July when watering should be reduced and feeding discontinued. Then repot and plunge in the garden, not in full sun, until it is brought indoors at the beginning of October.

When it is being repotted an Arum can be split up if the plant has grown too large. When growth begins, give more and more water and, occasionally, fertilizer.

SAINTPAULIA IONANTHA
African Violet

A modest little plant which resembles in shape and colour the wild violet. Not so long ago Saintpaulia was only to be found in hothouses and no one thought of bringing it into the dwelling house.

How it has happened that it is now on the market is hardly known but, in any case, it is seen throughout much of the year, especially in the summer months, when the florists have it in bloom and it is in great demand. At the moment there are even red and white varieties in commerce, but violet is the colour that has remained the favourite.

Saintpaulia, which comes from the Usambara Mountains, could just as well be called the Usambara or Cape Violet; it belongs to the same family as the *Gloxinia* and has nothing to do with violets. It is a particularly attractive plant with its dark green, oblong, round, hairy leaves, and hairy flower and leaf stalks, above which the blue-violet flowers appear for months on end.

The plant is usually purchased when in flower and should be given a light, warm position, for preference, not in the sun. In spring and summer shade it from the mid-day sun or for some hours put a piece of paper over it. If it is deprived of light for too long, it does not flower well and the buds may drop off. When flowering is over, give it less water, fertilizer every fortnight and then it can rest until the spring; it can be kept in a light place in a warm room at 60-65°F (16-18°C) and, if necessary, it can be given tepid water, preferably below in the ornamental pot. Keep it on the dry side during the winter, which will encourage flowering. If the plant flowers in the autumn, then put it under a lamp in the evening to lengthen the flowering period.

It is quite easy to propagate this plant by means of leaf cuttings. A fully grown leaf should be taken off with a short stalk and put into sandy soil. Fertilizer encourages the formation of roots. In an ordinary flower pot five leaves can be placed, which should be covered with glass or a plastic bag, and later replanted in a mixture of 1 part leaf-mould, 1 part woodland soil, some fertilizer and a little sharp sand. Between the middle of June and September, the leaf cuttings have the greatest chance of success at a temperature of 70-75°F (20-22°C).

SANSEVIERIA

Is there any other plant so well adapted as Sansevieria to modern styles of decoration?

Sansevieria is a curiously shaped plant, consisting of eight or ten leaves to each growth, which may reach a height of 2½-3 ft. (70-80 cm). They are typically sword-shaped, hence the common name, Wife's Tongue; the species *Sansevieria trifasciata* which comes from Indonesia, has greyish white bands across the leaves.

In the South African *Sansevieria trifasciata laurentii* the edges of the leaves are also coloured yellow, thereby increasing its beauty. Different in form is *Sansevieria trifasciata* '*Hahnii*' with the leaves in a rosette, as shown on the left of the illustration.

To keep the colour of the leaves, *Sansevieria* should have a light position and, in winter, a temperature of at least 60-65°F (15-18°C). Watering must be done very carefully in winter but in the summer, when it is growing, it wants plenty of water though care must be taken that none gets into the heart or it may rot. Every fortnight it wants fertilizer. In winter, tepid water should be given once a week and some people have considerable success using warm water in the saucer. In any case in summer and winter no water should be given if the soil looks dark and feels moist. Too much and too cold water causes the neck of the root to rot or brown spots to appear on the leaves.

It can be propagated by division of the plant or by leaf cuttings. In spring, preferably in April or May, the plant can be split up for which it should be taken out of the pot and the root stock cut through. It is best to take cuttings in the spring; a fully grown leaf is divided into pieces 2-4 in (5-10 cm) long; the cut surfaces are allowed to dry and then put into sharp sand at a temperature of 70°F (20°C) at least. After about a month, roots will probably have formed along the cut surfaces. They should then be potted up in a mixture of 2 parts turfy loam and 1 part leaf-mould, and do not forget the crocks at the bottom. The variety '*laurentii*' will give only green plants from cuttings; to retain the form with the beautiful markings, division of the plant is the only method.

Occasionally it produces long flowering stems with small, sweetly scented, white flowers. Cut the flower stems off after flowering.

SAXIFRAGA COTYLEDON *Saxifrage*

The name Saxifrage is mostly associated with garden plants, especially those for the rock garden and border.

Yet the decorative plant here illustrated, with its pyramid of flowers like a bridal bouquet, which is seen in the flower shops in May and June, is one of them. The name is *Saxifraga cotyledon pyramidalis* and it comes from the northern hemisphere so that it can be used as a garden plant.

Usually such a handsome plant is received in flower when, from the rosette of spatulate leaves, shining green in colour, a pyramid of flowers arises, 1½-2 ft. (40-60 cm) high, with countless fragrant, white stars, sometimes stippled with red.

Sometimes it is rather top-heavy and then the inflorescence should be tied to a small stick. It is sometimes seen hanging over the pot but this is not as it should be.

If the flowers begin to droop, it should be put out in the midday sun and given plenty of fresh air. While in flower it needs a lot of water, and fertilizer once a fortnight. It will be a disappointment when the plant dies after flowering but it makes young rosettes at the base of the mother plant, which can be removed and potted separately; these plants will flower in from 2-4 years.

It cannot be said with certainty that all the rosettes that have rooted will flower and so it is always wise to keep them separate and not all in one place. It can be seen later which ones are going to flower.

Since they grow best in sandy soil, preferably mixed with loam, they can be struck in this. First put them in a small pot to root and then transplant into a 4-inch pot which has a layer of crocks at the bottom. Before they are old enough to flower, the rosettes like full sun and fresh air.

In winter put them in a light, sunny room which is unheated but frost free. There they should be kept on the dry side and given no fertilizer.

Eventually, in the spring, give them a place in the sun or in half-shade and, when they show signs of flowering, they can be brought into the house but be careful that the change of position is made gradually.

If the flower spike droops, then soak the pot in a bucket of water up to the rim; during growth and flowering resume feeding and, once a week, water the pot well.

SCINDAPSUS *Pothos*

A modern climbing plant which can also be used as a trailer is *Scindapsus aureus,* often called *Pothos aureus,* by nurserymen. It is related to Philodendron and to the Arum Lily.

The leaves are fairly large, oblong and irregularly patterned with yellow, standing at right angles to the stem on very long, leaf stalks. The dark aerial roots, which are sometimes produced, are remarkable and even more so is the fact that the leaves, unlike those of most plants, are larger towards the top of the stem.

It is a tropical plant, used to warm surroundings and capable of standing the dry warmth produced by central heating. It does not need a light position, but the variegated markings on the leaves will last better in the light. The darker the position, the more readily will the markings be lost. It is particularly useful framing a window or door, or an arch between two rooms. The further it is from the light, the greater will be the distance between the leaves. It needs little water, so only water it when the soil is light in colour and feels dry. By using too much water or too cold, brown spots may appear on the leaves. Water at room temperature is recommended, especially in winter. Once a month give fertilizer throughout the year. The leaves may be sponged occasionally to keep them fresh but in the summer spray them now and then. Repotting is seldom necessary, only when the roots fill the pot; then use a mixture of leaf-mould, woodland soil, well-rotted manure or fertilizer and sharp sand. Do not forget to put crocks at the bottom. Top or side shoots about 4-6 in. (10-15 cm) long can be taken in spring or summer and rooted in a bottle of water, which should be kept in a dark place. When well rooted, pot them up in the mixture given above. In a light place, rooting is less rapid and less successful.

Yellow or brown coloured leaves with a web on the underside suggest red spider which should be treated by spraying with an insecticide. Repeat after 10-14 days or when necessary. Do not forget the underside of the leaves.

SOLANUM CAPSICASTRUM *Capsicum*

One of the brightest plants to appear in winter is Solanum, also known as Capsicum, with its round fruits among the dark green leaves. This Solanum comes from southern Brazil and belongs to the family *Solanaceae* or Nightshade and is, therefore, related to the Potato.

It is an evergreen shrub covered in autumn with strikingly coloured fruits which, with a little care, will remain on the bush for months on end. Provided it has plenty of water and a moist atmosphere produced, for example, by means of a steaming kettle or by leaving water to evaporate on the radiator, it is possible to keep the fruits in good condition; the drier the surroundings, the sooner they will shrivel up.

With central heating, daily spraying is necessary to prevent the leaves falling as well as the fruits drying up.

When the fruit is over, it is advisable to cut the plant down and to repot it in leaf-mould mixed with fertilizer and turf. In May Solanums can be put out of doors where the plants must be kept well watered and given fertilizer occasionally.

When it is growing well, care must be taken that the roots do not grow over the edge of the pot, for then the plant would make too much leaf and the flowers would not set fruit. By turning the plant regularly every three weeks, this can be prevented. To help the plant to set fruits it is better not to water over the plant during the flowering period which is August and September. If the tips are pinched out of the branches at the end of September, to prevent further growth, more and better fruit will result. At the beginning of October the plant is brought back into the house and put in a bright, cool place, where the atmosphere is rather moist for choice, to prevent the leaves dropping.

It can easily be raised from seed. In the spring, take the seeds out of the fruits that have fallen and sow them in a small pot and repot the young plants into a larger pot with the soil mixture as given above.

STEPHANOTIS *Bridal Flower*

The Bridal Flower, Stephanotis, like other tropical plants, is usually grown in a hot house. As the possibility of heating the dwelling house increases, the nurseryman can offer a wider range of plants. Many young wives, remembering their bridal bouquets, ask for this exotic climbing plant.

And so *Stephanotis floribunda,* which comes from Madagascar, is now found in many homes. It is a climbing plant with white, waxy, trumpet-shaped flowers in umbels in the leaf axils, which have a lily-like fragrance.

The nurseryman usually grows it in the ground in a hot house where it may reach a height of 12-15 ft. (4-5 m.) high. We buy a Stephanotis in a pot and train it up a pyramid of wire or canes.

When young it does not flower well but later, much more freely. The chief flowering period is from early summer to autumn. The best day temperature is between 55-65°F (12-18°C), whilst the temperature at night need not be higher than 60°F (15°C). It needs plenty of light and sun and, in summer, plenty of fresh air. In full sun at mid-day it may want shade for a few hours. The plant keeps its leaves during the winter and care should be taken that it does not dry out in the dry, warm atmosphere and is not attacked by pests. Put the pot on an inverted saucer in a bowl of water, so that the water does not touch the pot and, only by evaporation, the plant. Moreover, daily spraying is essential; during the growing and flowering periods the soil should be kept very moist. In winter on the other hand, too much water in the soil is wrong since it would result in the rotting of the root system.

Throughout the year use water at room temperature and, in winter, only tepid water for spraying.

In spring and summer fertilizer every fortnight is beneficial for growth and flowering. The plant wants a nourishing soil and when it outgrows its pot, it should be repotted in the spring in a mixture of leaf-mould, fertilizer and loam with sharp sand. In the spring, at the same time, cut out the branches that have flowered, otherwise the plant will grow too large.

Since Stephanotis may be attacked by mealy bug, scale and red spider it is advisable, as a preventive measure, to spray once a month with a solution of nicotine and soft soap. Mealy bug and scale can be treated with a brush dipped in methylated spirit.

STREPTOCARPUS

One of the prettiest of the plants that flower in summer is the Streptocarpus which, like *Gloxinia,* belongs to the *Gesneriaceae,* as is obvious from the form of the flowers. They, also, are bell-shaped but more delicate in form with slender stalks arising from the axils of the leaves. The leaves are grooved on the upper side, light green and oblong, mostly arranged in a rosette. There are lovely colours amongst the hybrids such as dark blue, pink, lilac, pure white and white veined in purple. The plants are unbelievably prolific, last a long time and give much pleasure in the house. If well cared for, their lovely flowers can be enjoyed for three months in the summer and the plant can easily be grown on for another year.

Streptocarpus should be given a light position but not in the sun and throughout the summer it should be watered regularly. In a dry atmosphere pests may occur which can be removed by treatment such as spraying with soft soap and methylated spirit in water. After 10-14 days repeat when necessary. In the autumn when the flowers are over, keep it drier and when the leaves are dry, Streptocarpus should be kept dry in the pot also at a temperature not below 45°F (6°C).

In spring (February to March) when it reappears, the plant should be repotted and when this is done, the plant will want no fertilizer for the rest of the year. Since the plant is tender, it does not need feeding but is undoubtedly better in fresh soil. For repotting use leaf-mould, fertilizer, peat and sharp sand. Then keep it at 60-65°F (16-18°C).

Although nurserymen usually raise them from seed, it is also possible from cuttings. In February or March a fully grown leaf is divided into pointed pieces and these put into a box of loam and sand; cover with glass and keep evenly moist. Put them on the mantelpiece or radiator. As soon as a heart develops, put the little plants into pots in the soil mixture given above.

SYNGONIUM

The Syngoniums are natives of tropical virgin forests in South America and related to *Monstera deliciosa* and the countless *Philodendrons.* They are lianes which, by means of their stems, wind round their support, and produce a large number of aerial roots.

Syngonium auritum is distinguished by its finger-like leaves, sometimes likened to a rabbit's head, on long leaf stalks. There are also types with smaller, finger-like leaves and a creeping habit such as *Syngonium podophyllum* and therefore appropriate for a garden frame.

On account of its tropical origin and as a shade lover, Syngoniums need a warm position and shade from the sun. They do not like being by a window but prefer to be further into the room, hall or passage, provided it is warmed in winter, and not below 60°F (15°C) and free from draughts.

They need a constantly moist warmth. The small-leaved Syngoniums thrive very well in winter on the corner of a warm mantelpiece.

A moist atmosphere can be obtained by putting the pot on an inverted saucer, so that the water does not reach the pot, or to put some damp moss on the pot and also between the pot and the ornamental one surrounding it. The plant itself wants a lot of water which should not be cold, and in winter, warmer than the temperature of the room. Sponge the leaves weekly and several times a week, especially in the winter, spray overhead. In spring and summer fertilizer can be given every fortnight but if the growth is too vigorous, reduce to once a month. In winter feeding is stopped altogether. If the plant gets too tall, the tips can be cut off and parts of the stem used as cuttings. Eventually aerial roots will form on the underside. They should be put in leaf-mould and sharp sand covered with a plastic bag or put in a warm, light place. When the cuttings are growing well, then give them a stronger soil mixture of leaf-mould, fertilizer, sharp sand and some peat.

Owing to the dry heat of sunshine in the summer, red spider may occur, recognisable by the yellow or brown flecks and sometimes a web on the underside of the leaf. For treatment, see *Ficus elastica.*

THUNBERGIA ALATA *Black-eyed Susan*

In the last few years a new indoor plant has made its appearance, the climber *Thunbergia alata,* which comes from South-east Africa.

In practice it is generally treated as an annual since, even if it did last longer, it is seldom that it has survived the winter in a house. In a greenhouse it does very well because there is always plenty of light and sun with moderate warmth.

Thunbergia can be raised from seed sown in February or March. It is sown in boxes or pots, with crocks or gravel at the bottom and filled with sieved leaf-mould and sharp sand. It is a good thing to have the upper inch (3 cm) filled with sieved leaf-mould only. The pot is filled to within about $\frac{3}{4}$ in. (2 cm) below the rim; press the soil down with the hand and scatter the seed all over the surface. Then press the seeds down and, if necessary add a little more soil. Water it with a syringe and cover with glass. Put it in a warm room and lay paper over it until the seeds start to germinate, about 2-3 weeks. Then put it in the sun, keep it moist and give more and more light. When they are large enough to handle, put the plantlets separately into pots. Give them plenty of sun and fresh air. Thunbergia is not exacting, but it has a preference for calcareous soil.

It needs support when it is beginning to hang down but it can absorb more light if it is trained upwards, by means of sticks round the edge of the pot or a hoop can be made of wire.

Thunbergia wants plenty of light and, in the summer, plenty of fresh air. In some sheltered, sunny gardens it can be grown out of doors during the summer months but the chances of its living on are not great. By the beginning of July, in any case, it is better not to try. It wants plenty of water on the soil, but not when this is dark in colour and feels damp. Give fertilizer once a week. A well-grown plant may reach a height of 3-6 ft. (1-2 m).

In general it develops better if the pot is plunged in a flower stand or a box in soil, when it will not dry out so quickly. Flowering may begin in May or June and last into the New Year, but on account of the poor light then, give it a sunny position.

TRADESCANTIA *Wandering Jew*

An old fashioned hanging plant which has retained its popularity through the years is Tradescantia; it is used as ground work in floral arrangements or on the corner of the window sill from which its slender stems hang gracefully down.

It is a very easy plant to grow in a room and is, in consequence, apt to be neglected or put in a dark corner as it is thought that any position will do. But it cannot grow without light and should be kept out of the mid-day sun. The sturdiest kind is the ordinary green form but it is not so attractive as some of the other varieties which all have more or less beautifully coloured leaves. The plant most often met with is *Tradescantia fluminensis (Tradescantia repens)* whose green leaves are striped and edged with silvery white. A similar plant is *Tradescantia blossfeldiana* with boat-shaped, dark green leaves, purple on the underside, and trusses of tripartite, lilac flowers in the summer. It can stand full sun and wants plenty of water. The plants in the illustration are, at the back from left to right *Zebrina purpusii, Tradescantia blossfeldiana* and *Tradescantia albiflora 'Albo vittata'*. In front on the left *Tradescantia albiflora,* right *Zebrina pendula.*

A characteristic of Tradescantia is that it indicates itself how much light it wants for, if it is in too dark a place, then gradually the lovely colouring of the leaves disappears and it reverts to the original green. Close to it is the now much grown *Setcreasea* (the leaves covered with violet hairs). In summer it needs plenty of water and fertilizer as well as fresh air. In winter keep it cool and on the dry side.

The more beautifully the leaf is coloured, the warmer it should be kept in the winter, but the atmosphere must not be too moist. On older plants which overhang their pots the leaves may wither. Cut off the tips and use them as cuttings by putting pieces 3-4 in. (6-10 cm) long in a pot 5 in. (12 cm) in diameter, and in a month or two they will make good plants. A suitable soil mixture consists of 1 part leaf-mould, 1 part turfy loam and 1 part sand; when the cuttings are growing give them fertilizer every fortnight from May to November.

VRIESEA *Bromeliad*

The long flat flower spike of *Vriesea splendens major* looks like a flash of lightening rising from the splendid rosette of striped leaves. Even if it does not flower, this South American Bromeliad is a very worth-while house plant. The leaf is leathery, dark green and marbled in dark purple and, as in all the Bromeliads, the leaves form a funnel-shaped rosette, overlapping each other.

The inflorescence, shaped like an ear of corn, generally appears in spring and consists of scales arranged like tiles overlapping each other, which are more striking than the tiny yellow flowers.

It is not very common, possibly because it wants a constant temperature and moist atmopshere. A temperature of 65-70°F (18-20°C) is sufficient in winter. It can stand some sun but, for choice, it should be in the morning sun only and in the summer it should be shaded from the sun at mid-day or moved to some other light place.

In summer it wants plenty of water, which should be at room temperature and given water regularly poured into the leaf rosette. In nature when growing on trees, it catches in this leaf sheath both water and food; at one time the soil only was given water by growers but then the plant does not flower. If water is poured into the sheath then the flower stem can develop. When this can be seen, it is better to stop watering into the sheath which might, when the plant is indoors, cause the stem to rot. In houses with central heating, watering into the sheath can be continued in the winter, if the night temperature does not fall too low. During the growing and flowering period Vriesea should be given fertilizer every fortnight.

Like all Bromeliads, it flowers once and then dies. But, in the meantime, young shoots will have formed from the root, which are not yet large enough to flower. So, after flowering, cut out the flower stalk and give fertilizer as soon as the young plants are half the size of the mother plant which should later be taken out of the ground and the little plants cut off, if possible with a few roots attached to each.

Put them into small pots with a layer of crocks at the bottom and use a light compost of 3 parts leaf-mould, 1 part sphagnum and 1 part fertilizer. The old plant is of no further use.

ZYGOCACTUS *Epiphyllum, Christmas Cactus*

This Cactus, which is so unlike the usual idea of a Cactus, flowers about Christmas time, when flowering plants are so welcome. The flowers are rather like those of a Fuchsia with their crimson bells and the petals spreading out like ballet skirts, surrounding the large bunch of stamens.

Sometimes the plant is acquired in bud and then, more often than not, a number of the buds fall off, which is usually due to the fact that the plant has been jolted too much, or turned round, for this Cactus, whose flowers always turn to the light, needs to be kept in the same position. Above all it will not stand great fluctuations of temperature between day and night. Coming from Brazil where it lives on branches and tree trunks in the mountain forests, it is accustomed to little sun and plenty of water during the rainy period from April to September.

Indoors also it must be shaded from direct sunlight in spring and summer but should be as near the window as possible. Whilst in flower give it plenty of water and fertilizer once a fortnight, and when the resting period begins, the plant should be put in a cool place, given little water and no feeding until April when it can be treated as before.

It is a good thing to put the plant out in the garden during the summer, where it should be given the same treatment as in the house. Bring it indoors again in September, in a light room at 60-65°F (16-18°C), where it should be given little water and no fertilizer until the buds have formed and then it can be put back into its permanent position and not moved again. A fully grown joint can be treated as a cutting in the spring or summer, but if three or four joints together are used as a cutting the new plant will flower earlier. Leave it to dry for several days. Put the cutting into sand and later replant in a rich soil of leaf-mould, sand and fertilizer, good garden soil and turfy loam. Repot the Christmas cactus as seldom as possible otherwise it will not flower so well.

INDEX

Including Latin and Popular English Names.